ECONOQUAKE!

HOW TO SURVIVE AND PROSPER
IN THE COMING
GLOBAL DEPRESSION

BARRY HOWARD MINKIN

ECONO-QUAKE

HOW TO SURVIVE & PROSPER IN THE COMING GLOBAL DEPRESSION

PRENTICE HALL
Englewood Cliffs, New Jersey 07632

Prentice-Hall International (UK) Limited, *London*
Prentice-Hall of Australia Pty. Limited, *Sydney*
Prentice-Hall Canada, Inc., *Toronto*
Prentice-Hall Hispanoamericana, S.A., *Mexico*
Prentice-Hall of India Private Limited, *New Delhi*
Prentice-Hall of Japan, Inc., *Tokyo*
Simon & Schuster Asia Pte. Ltd., *Singapore*
Editora Prentice-Hall do Brasil, Ltda., *Rio de Janeiro*

© 1993 *by*
PRENTICE-HALL, Inc.
Englewood Cliffs, NJ

This book is sold with the understanding that neither the writer
or publisher is engaged in rendering legal, accounting or
securities services. Questions relevant to those practices should
be addressed to a member of those professions.

The author and publisher specifically disclaim any liability, loss,
or risk, personal or otherwise, which is incurred as a
consequence, directly or indirectly, of the use and application of
any of the contents of this work. The author or company he
controls may from time to time have either long or short
positions in the securities recommended in this book.

Econoquake, Econo-2000 strategic and forecasting models,
Light- Dark psychographic, and America 2000 are trademarks
of Minkin Affiliates.

10 9 8 7 6 5 4 3 2 1

Library of Congress Cataloging–in–Publication Data

Minkin, Barry Howard.
    Econoquake! how to survive and prosper in the coming global
depression/Barry Howard Minkin.
        p.   cm.
    Includes index.

    ISBN 0–13–224866–2
    1. Economic forecasting—United States.   2. United States—
Economic conditions—1981–   3. Depressions—United States.
4. Investments—United States.   I. Title.
HC106.8.M573 1993
330.973'0928—dc20   92-33486
                                                            CIP

ISBN 0-13-224866-2

PRENTICE HALL
Professional Publishing
Englewood Cliffs, NJ 07632
Simon & Schuster. A Paramount Communications Company

PRINTED IN THE UNITED STATES OF AMERICA

❦

For: Miss Reba, Brett, and Melissa
and in loving memory of Isidore "Joe" Minkin

❦

ACKNOWLEDGMENTS

Thanks first to Tom Power for having the vision and courage to champion this book.

Hats off to Dave Riley, Anne Knight, Patricia Blumenthal, and Victor Eydus for their first rate editing and to Scott Sloan for excellent graphics.

Special thanks to John Cardis for his support, editing, and advice.

Thanks to Tom Peters, Hugh Crane, Bob Lee, Putney Westerfield, Dave Nee, John Petrick, Ed Wingeth, Gene Biggi, Joe Grippo, Jim Rosen, Greg Steltenpohl, Joe McPherson, Jack Painter, Dudley Andersen, James Q. Wilson, Al Petterson, Norman Glickman, and Douglas Woodward, Phil Umholtz, Carl Minkin, Melissa Minkin, and all the others who supplied me with material included in book. Thanks as well to the Jackson Library of the Stanford Graduate School of Business and the Bay Area libraries for their cooperation and assistance.

Thanks to Camp Pevey for sharing his computer wisdom and to Don Cresswell, Nancy Karp, Charles Turk, Joel Goldfus, and Stephen Minkin for their early contributions in helping to formulate my ideas and to

Dan Stucker for his help with endnotes, index and permissions.

Final thanks go to all friends and loved ones whose support and love sustained me and I can finally return now that my message is delivered.

INTRODUCTION

There is no rest for a messenger till the message is delivered.

Joseph Conrad

He's naked!

**Hans Christian Andersen,
in "The Emperor's New Clothes"**

This book may depress and scare you, but it may also save your financial future. Right now the United States seems to be slowly pulling out of a recession that has lasted much longer and has been much deeper than many of the so-called "experts" ever predicted. Everyone, from top-level managers to department store clerks, is worrying about his or her job. Businesses are subsisting hand-to-mouth, waiting for the recovery to get going in earnest.

But They May Be Waiting for a Long Time

I predict that the U.S. economy, which is linked to the economies of most countries, is soon to collapse into a depression that will be similar in many ways to that of the 1930s. Hundreds of companies will go bankrupt. Real estate markets, already down by 30% in some areas, will go into free-fall. Unemployment will reach 15%, putting many middle class families out on the streets. Retirees will find their investments and pensions turning to dust.

This won't happen all at once. For a while, perhaps as long as a year, a recovery may appear to have started, as it did in 1927, when a mild recession had apparently been checked by easing of the credit situation. But by mid-1994, growth will stall, businesses will keep cutting costs by laying off workers, and scared consumers will stop spending, making business conditions even worse. The resulting recession will prove quite different from the one we're leaving but very similar to the recession that preceded the stock market collapse at the end of October 1929. The 1994 recession, like the one in 1929, will not respond to government monetary policies.

By the last quarter of 1994, the U.S. economy will react as if it's been hit by an econoquake—a tremendous shaking of the economic landscape that will leave a ruin of economically crippled businesses and individuals across the country.

Who's to Blame?

Why do I tell these tales of gloom, when even the most pessimistic of economists sees growth in the 1990s? As an advisor since the 1970s to some of the world's largest businesses, I've been seeing the impending signs of disaster for years. The U.S. economy is only as sound as its big companies, and they've turned into a bunch of losers—fat, arthritic elephants that have been preserved only by sheer inertia and their great size.

Just look at the facts. After spending over $100 billion, U.S. automakers are still losing ground to the Japanese. The big-money central banks like Chase Manhattan and Continental Illinois, once powerhouses feared the world over, are struggling to survive. And even America's pride and joy, the computer industry, is in trouble. Over the last two years, the large computer manufacturers have laid off roughly 200,000 workers, and even IBM is suffering contraction pangs. For much of the 1980s, the magnitude of these problems was papered over. America's population was growing at a rate of 1% annually, providing easy markets. Japanese and European investors were willing to pour money into U.S. real estate and factories. And the newly industrialized countries needed the U.S. consumer to buy the output of the efficient factories in Japan, Taiwan, and Korea.

But now, population growth at home has stopped. Foreign companies burned by the real estate crash and such well-publicized disasters as Bridgestone's acquisition of Firestone are finding better places to spend their money. Our costs were often too high and our quality too low for the United States to be a successful producer, and our emptying wallets are also making us increasingly irrelevant as consumers.

True, almost every chief executive officer of a *Fortune* 500 company is proclaiming publicly that once the recession and pain of "restructuring" are over, prosperity will be just around the corner. The auto industry is forecasting that it's going to sell 13.5 million cars and light trucks in 1992, twice last year's total. Even the steel industry, battered by imports, is predicting profitability once the recession ends.

But for all their rosy predictions, insiders know that their companies are in deep trouble. For many companies, 1990 will turn out to have been their peak sales year. That's why they're still cutting workers, even though economists claim that the recession is ending. For a few lucky companies, that sort of slimming down may work, but for most of them, it's too late. Even when the elephant loses weight and is lighter on its feet, it still can't dance.

Today's state of affairs is the result of years of consistently wrong decisions, such as the lack of investment. Leaving out the computer industry, investment fell flat in the 1980s. And even when money was spent, it was spent poorly. Too many dollars have gone into decorating that should have gone into substance. For example, department stores spend billions each year to redecorate and remodel, and Ford spends $600 million for a simple car redesign; our international competitors, however, are investing in modern assembly plants.

There is no single savior, not even high technology. In truth, the biggest failure of the 1980s was the failure of the computer industry to generate more jobs. In fact, as measured by the Bureau of Labor Statistics, the number of computer-related manufacturing jobs actually shrank. And there are no new businesses to save the day.

The Mistaken Forecasts

The so-called "experts," the economists and big-picture types, don't see the depths of our problems. This is because they haven't been looking in the right places. By focusing solely on the "big picture," they're overlooking the fact that the ground we're all standing on is shaky. Even the pessimists are looking in the wrong direction. They've been looking for a cyclical financial collapse when the real problem is the collapse of our industrial base (see Chapter 1).

But if you truly acknowledge that an econoquake is coming, you can prepare yourself, and your investments, and can escape much of the damage. Indeed, the econoquake will set in motion a massive redistribution of wealth in the world, so it's a good time to make money investing in troubled times.

All Doom and Gloomers Are Not Alike

I can understand feeling skeptical about the coming of a major depression. Experts have cried "wolf" before. I had no intention of being an economic prognosticator, and I truly dislike bringing bad news. But, as I discuss in Chapter 5, in the 1970s a light went on for me when, as a management consultant working with scores of companies in our industrial heartland, I realized that the longest and deepest recession since World War II was caused by the coincidence of particular company- and industry-specific structural variables. They had almost nothing to do with business cycles, inflation, money supply, or most other indicators that economists consider from their ivy towers.

In the past, most writers of "doom-and-gloom" books have also made their predictions by using the tools and language of traditional economics. That is precisely why their predictions have mostly been off the mark. You wouldn't expect a lawyer to understand why a building's plumbing system isn't working. If you have a plumbing problem, you call a plumber. Yet to understand the inner workings of our diverse industries, we have been listening to economists, many of whom have worked only as university professors, and to politicians, most of whom are lawyers. This is tantamount to trying to fix leaks with the wrong tools.

In my more than 25 years as a management consultant, I've solved problems for scores of companies and governments worldwide. This has given me a real-world perspective on where we are today, how we got there, and where we are heading.

I understand and encourage skepticism about what I've written, for I am quite aware that it runs counter to mainstream economic thought, the optimistic forecasts of well-respected futurists, and even the views of some contributors to this book. I therefore recommend that you discuss the implications of my views with your advisors. But whatever your views, I strongly recommend that you read this short book, which explains why I think a major depression is inevitable and how to survive and prosper through the tough times ahead. Whether or not you agree with my rationale and conclusions, I'm sure you'll find some valuable tips on investing, jobs, education, demographics, business, and other important topics.

Oh, Well, at Least It Can't Get Worse

In Bernard Malamud's novel *The Fixer,* the protagonist experiences ever-deeper levels of despair in a Russian dungeon as his captors continuously crush his hopes.[1] This emotional whirlpool of a narrative leaves the reader saying to himself at the end of each chapter, "Well, it can't get much worse." In fact, it does, but still Malamud's protagonist survives. So it is with the econoquake. After part one of this book opens your eyes to the negative economic reality that is now unfolding, part two features suggestions from a variety of experts on ways we can survive and even prosper.

ENDNOTES

1.   Bernard Malamud, *The Fixer* (New York, NY: Farrar, Straus, and Giroux).

ABOUT THE AUTHOR

With over 25 years of global management consulting experience, including 10 years with Stanford Research Institute (now SRI International), Barry Minkin has worked with scores of companies of all sizes and across most industry sectors. His insights into the company-specific factors that determine success in the real world have allowed him to accurately develop market and economic forecasts for his clients. As his reputation for accurate forecasting grew, he was asked to publish his forecasts in the *Corporate Times* in Silicon Valley. His regular monthly column, *Future-In-Sight,* contained dozens of specific predictions ranging from high-tech to high-touch. For example, he was the first person to predict the decline of the semiconductor industry in the 1980s, as well as predicting the success of *Trivial Pursuit* before the first game was sold in the United States.

He holds an M.B.A. degree from the Bernard Baruch School of the City University of New York. He has received numerous awards, including the American Society for Training and Development Achievement Award, and a Presidential Citation for Innovative Employment of the Handicapped. He is listed in the directory of *Merger and Acquisition Professionals, Who's Who of Dealmakers, Who's Who in the East, and Who's Who in the West.* He is a certified business opportunity appraiser, and licensed business broker. He is often quoted, and has been a regular on radio, T.V., and in local newspapers, and has been a guest speaker for numerous associations and corporations.

To request information regarding the Econoquake newsletter and seminars, or acquisition, market analysis, strategic planning, and consulting services for businesses, government, and individuals, write to:

Minkin Affiliates
617 Forest Avenue
Palo Alto, CA 94301
or FAX:
415-323-2950

CONTENTS

INTRODUCTION   ix

**PART ONE   The Econoquake: Why It's Inevitable;
What Will Happen**

Chapter 1 The Econoquake:
The Economic Bust of the 1990s   1

Chapter 2 The Global Employment Bust
of the 1990s   17

Chapter 3 Chilly Investment Climate
of the 1990s   37

Chapter 4 Broken-Down Engines   55

Chapter 5 Economists and Other Pundits:
Why the Experts Are Missing It   77

PART TWO Implications, Recommendations, and   Opportunities

Chapter 6 How the Econoquake
              Will Change Society   97

Chapter 7 Business Implications and Growth
              Opportunities   113

Chapter 8 Investing in an Econoquake   147

Chapter 9 Jobs and Education
              in an Econoquake   179

Chapter 10 Reversing the Tide: Policies for
              Rebuilding After the Econoquake   211

INDEX   255

PART I

The Econoquake:
Why It's Inevitable;
What Will Happen

THE ECONOQUAKE: THE ECONOMIC BUST OF THE 1990s

Scientists assure us that California, where I've lived for the last two decades, will be hit by another big earthquake soon. Over the next five or ten years, the San Andreas fault or some other unstable piece of the earth's crust will slip, and millions of dollars of California real estate will disintegrate in a matter of a few seconds. Still, people continue to build homes perched perilously on the side of hills. They pretend the big quake won't happen or hope that, if it does, it will miss them.

   This is not a book about geology; it is about economics. But the earthquake serves as an excellent metaphor for what is going on throughout the world today. We are now in the early stage of an economic earthquake—I call it "an econoquake"—that will arrive by the end of 1994. Unfortunately, economic forecasters and other prognosticators are choosing to ignore the evidence before their eyes. The economy is riddled with fault lines, and the pressures on them have been building for too long. Slippage toward economic rupture has already begun. The biggest problem is that there are so many weaknesses in the economy, it's impossible for the president, the Federal Reserve, or Congress to patch all of them.

If you still have doubts that an econoquake is coming, this chapter should eliminate them. In this chapter, I'm going to point out the four deepest and most damaging fault lines. Once you've seen them, you'll understand why an econoquake is inevitable.

FAULT LINE 1:
America's Lack of International Competitiveness

True, we still make most of the world's commercial aircraft, and we have a few other products that inspire the world to "buy American." But for the most part, we buy much more than we sell on world markets, and we borrow to make up the difference. And like any debtor in hock to the neighborhood loan shark, we're finding more and more of our income going to pay off old debts.

The numbers don't lie. In the 1980s the United States ran up a net merchandise trade deficit of $1.04 trillion. How did we finance all these videocassette recorders (VCRs), imported cars, and barrels of oil? Simple. We borrowed, and borrowed big—from the Saudis, the Kuwaitis, the Germans, the Japanese, and any other prosperous foreigners who would lend to us. According to the official statistics, about $143 billion of the U.S. government debt is owned by foreigners. The true figure may be much higher than the government will admit.

What this means is that the United States is shipping an awful lot of money abroad to pay interest on our debts. Let's examine the consequences. Assume that foreigners lent us money at 8%, which was the average interest rate in the 1980s. On a foreign-owned debt of $143 billion, that adds up to more than $11 billion being turned over to foreigners, in annual interest charges alone. *To put it in a different way, $11 billion would be enough to close most of the state and local budget gaps.*

The White House would have us believe we're on the road to recovery, but the fact is that we're still running big trade deficits and still borrowing to pay for them. In 1991, a comparatively good year, U.S. consumers, businesses, and governments bought $73 billion more in foreign goods than they sold overseas. Once again, what we're doing is living like a profligate, borrowing not only to buy new goods, but worse, borrowing to pay off old debts while still living beyond our means. Treasury auctions have become a kind of national debt consolidation loan.

We got into this hole as the result of an incredibly flawed policy promulgated by the White House in the mid–1980s. As the U.S. trade deficit mounted, the Reagan administration was under pressure to restore the balance of trade advantage the United States had enjoyed as recently as the 1970s. To do so it relied on an overly simplistic economic monetary dogma: weaken the U.S. dollar, and you restore competitiveness by making our goods less expensive overseas and making foreign goods more expensive here. On the surface, it seemed that it would work. The U.S. strategy sharply cut the dollar's value against the mark, yen, and pound. The yen dropped most precipitously, from almost 250 to about 120.

But this strategy, devised at a September 1985 meeting at the Plaza Hotel in New York, unwittingly played right into the hands of the other industrialized countries participating in the conference. The weak U.S. dollar has not produced the hoped-for improvement in the trade deficit, primarily because the reasons we haven't been selling more goods overseas obviously have little to do with the value of anybody's currency. What this devaluation actually—and disastrously—did was to give foreigners more money to spend in the United States. For the Japanese, it was the equivalent of a half-price going-out-of-business sale on anything they wanted to buy in the United States.

As a management consultant during the 1980s, I soon became aware of a change in the business focus of my Japanese clients. Discussions regarding trade and licensing of U.S. products were scrapped, and the focus switched to identifying companies and real estate that the Japanese could acquire. Why buy milk when the cow is cheap? Indeed, the Reagan dollar policy goof moved large foreign companies from all over the globe to acquire ownership of American companies. By 1989, foreign investment in the United States had reached $2 trillion. Billion-dollar-plus acquisitions of U.S. companies had become commonplace.

Table 1-1 displays billion-dollar-plus acquisitions for the three years following the Plaza Accord.

Some people argue that it doesn't matter who owns American companies. If they are operating in the United States, they are contributing to our economy. But the fact is that foreign-owned companies can do a lot more juggling of their books than can Ford, IBM, or Bank of America. As a result, they pay far less in U.S. taxes than American-owned companies, which aggravates our budget deficit. By one estimate, the United States is losing billions in taxes each year as a result of foreign ownership. Moreover, instead of contributing to our growth, the profits from these foreign companies are being spent offshore improving their owners' respective national economies.

And foreign-owned plants in the United States are not the answer. In the auto industry, for example, 40% of the cars the Japanese sell in the United States are built here. However, studies show these so-called "transplants" may actually hurt us more than they help. The Japanese import the most expensive parts and buy many other components from Japanese suppliers. The net result is that the Japanese-owned U.S. auto manufacturers eliminate more jobs than they create.

The Economic Strategy Institute, a Washington-based trade policy group, credits the transplants with

TABLE 1-1 Billion-Dollar Plus Acquisitions of U.S. Companies, 1986–1988

ACQUISTION	BUYER	
Celanese	Hoechst	(Germany)
Container Corp of America	Jefferson Smurfit	(Ireland)
CBS Records	Sony	(Japan)
Chesebrough-Ponds	Unilever	(Netherlands)
Kidde	Hanson Trust	(United Kingdom)
Heublein	Grand Met	(United Kingdom)
Manpower	Blue Arrow	(United Kingdom)
Federated Department Stores	Campeau	(Canada)
Pillsbury	Grand Met	(United Kingdom)
Farmers Group	B.A.T.	(United Kingdom)
Triangle Publications	News Corporation	(Australia)
Macmillan	Maxwell	(United Kingdom)
Firestone	Bridgestone	(Japan)
Intercontinental Hotel	Seibu/Saison Group	(Japan)
Koppers	Beazer	(United Kingdom)
Triangle Industries	Pechiney	(France)
Gould	Nippon Mining	(France)
Big Three Industries	L'Air Liquide	(France)

SOURCE: Adapted by Minkin Affiliates from *The New Competitors; How Foreign Investors Are Changing the U.S. Economy*, Norman J. Glickman/Douglas Woodward, by Basic Books, Inc., a division of Harper Collins Publishers, Inc.

creating 41,154 jobs and contributing $2.9 billion to the U.S. economy. However, when one considers that 70% of the transplants in fact displaced sales of Big Three car models, the lower domestic content of the transplants caused a loss of 124,355 U.S. jobs and a loss of $9.2 billion to the U.S. gross national product (GNP). The bottom line: the transplants caused a net loss of 83,000 U.S. jobs and a loss of $6.3 billion to U.S. GNP.

FAULT LINE 2:
The Stagnation and Consolidation of U.S. Business Sectors

There's little hope that this trend will be reversed anytime soon, since much of U.S. industry has given up the fight or was never in the battle to begin with. Our manufacturing industries are in maturing low-growth markets, and we have no new markets to take up the slack.

Take consumer electronics, a $70 billion industry. As a consequence of decisions made years ago by NBC, RCA, General Electric, and others, no TV sets are currently built in the United States. As for radios, VCRs, and portable tape players, the companies that could be making them failed, went out of business, or shipped thousands of jobs to Mexico and the Far East.

The case of the automobile industry is even more distressing. The Big Three automakers have benefited from ten years of protection from Japanese imports, enabling them to keep prices high. They've used the money to invest billions on reseach and development (R&D) and new plants and equipment. GM alone has spent billions over the last ten years, representing a sizable fraction of total U.S. nondefense R&D spending.

Yet the Japanese are still building a better, cheaper car. If you want proof, don't turn to the *Congressional Record,* turn to this year's *Consumer Report's Buying Guide.* Ford may say "Quality Is Job Number 1" and Iaccoca may say "Chrysler is listening to consumers,"

but the ultimate experts, American car buyers, are saying something else. In *Consumer Report's* category "Predicted Reliability," model after model of American car is
rated "much worse than average," while their Japanese
counterparts are rated "much better than average." The
numbers show that quality counts with consumers. In
1990, auto and auto parts accounted for 75% of our trade
deficit with Japan.

"For years, I thought what was good for the country
was good for General Motors and vice versa," GM President Charles Wilson said in 1952, and he was right. During 1988-89, the most recent prerecession peak, the auto
industry was directly responsible for 4% of the U.S.
GNP. Even more meaningful is that the 1.65 million
auto industry jobs represent more employment than offered by any other manufacturing industry.

After the government, General Motors is the
nation's largest purchaser of office furniture and personal computers. The auto industry also buys an enormous share of U.S. raw materials. It consumes over 60%
of malleable iron and lead, 18% of the aluminum, and
12% of the U.S. steel. It uses almost 80% of the rubber
and 25% of all the glass we consume as a nation. It uses
40% of machine tools and over half our screw machines
and stampings. A surprising 20% of all the semiconductors produced by the high-tech sector is purchased by
the auto industry.

Moreover, the health of numerous U.S. industries is
dependent on the auto industry. Indeed, the automobile
industry is a core industry that directly and indirectly
affects countless companies throughout the economy,
creating 12.87 million jobs. Every auto job creates 7.8
jobs in other industries.

However, because the U.S. auto industry failed to
perceive or respond to a changed marketplace in a
timely manner and build an inexpensive quality car, it
has become the epicenter of fault lines streaking across

the industrial heartland. Breadwinners from many other industries and their families are suffering from failures on the part of Big Three management and labor.

If 7.8 jobs are lost in other industries for every auto industry job lost, the planned layoff announced in 1992 of 74,000 at GM could put out of work over a half million people. Given the failing health of Chrysler and the continued erosion of the share of the auto market controlled by the United States, you can begin to understand why an econoquake is inevitable.

But perhaps you believe that the service sector or high technology will save the day. The service sector includes airlines and other forms of transportation, construction, real estate, public utilities, wholesale and retail trade, finance, insurance, banks, hospitals, restaurants, and similar industries. In the 1980s, it started to expand at a rapid rate, attracting tremendous amounts of foreign and domestic capital. That was particularly good news for the United States, because the vast majority of its domestic jobs lay in the service sector. But when financiers and builders found they had enormously overbuilt and were stuck with vacant buildings on which they owed huge construction loans, the service sector became part of the problem rather than the solution to a troubled economy. The ripple effect quickly turned into a tidal wave. Bank after bank has failed as a result of unsound construction lending, and millions of consumers have lost billions of dollars when a much heralded wealth builder of the 1980s, the real estate investment trust (REIT), proved untrustworthy.

So when manufacturing and service failed to serve as the engines to power the economy, the United States seemed left with one last hope: high tech. But high technology has turned out not to be a major employer, particularly of blue-collar workers. Moreover, like so many other industries, today it's shrinking. Giant IBM has broken a decades-old promise to its employees by finally uttering the "L" word—layoff. Apple Computer, which actually enjoys an enviable cash position and until recently claimed it had no long-term debt, is also reducing jobs to remain competitive.

The problems of trade deficit and unemployment are not going to go away soon, since even in the newest technologies, the United States is lagging. According to the Council on Competitiveness, we're way behind in one-third of the key cutting-edge technologies. The most horrifying example of our technological tardiness: liquid crystal displays (LCD). These are found on most notebook computers, and they will power the television sets of the future. Sharp of Japan is the acknowledged LCD leader, and there are only a couple of very small U.S. companies struggling to keep up. Companies like IBM are forced to go abroad to buy their displays, dropping even more dollars offshore.

That's not just a fault line, it's a chasm, because for every job eliminated in manufacturing or high technology, at least one and probably many more jobs in the service sector are reduced or eliminated.

A major contributor to the growing army of unemployed is the unprecedented rash of corporate mergers, acquisitions, consolidations, and bankruptcies. A significant part of my consulting practice involves identifying acquisition candidates for companies worldwide. The practice has allowed me a wide perspective of the rapidly narrowing industrial landscape.

Corporate megamergers are occurring in all industry sectors; Table 1-2 displays large mergers and acquisitions by U.S. companies over the past three years. These consolidations present a serious and long-range problem that will become an icy downhill slope for U.S. employment for years to come, as we shall see shortly.

True, mergers seem necessary and helpful in many industries. With about 12,000 banks nationwide, we have many more than we need. It has been argued that

**TABLE 1-2 Large Mergers and Acquisitions by U.S.
Companies, 1989–1991**

INDUSTRY	ORGANIZATION	TRANSACTION
Banking	Bank of America and Security Pacific	Merger
	Chemical Bank and Manufacturers Hanover	Announced merger
Airlines	United and Pan Am	Acquires Pan Am London routes
	American and TWA	Acquires TWA London routes
Appliances	Maytag and Chicago Pacific (Hoover Vacuum)	Acquisition
Software	Ashton-Tate and Borland	Merger
	Novell and Digital Research	Merger

SOURCE: Business Week/Minkin Affiliates

we need to consolidate them to compete with foreign megabanks for global markets. And many institutions with dwindling capital due to bad loans and mismanagement need to merge or be acquired before they are added to the rising numbers of bank failures. The likely removal of the roadblocks to interstate banking also suggest that consolidation of banks would be helpful.

But consolidations will become major contributors to the econoquake. In 1991, the top four announced bank mergers could eliminate approximately 25,000 jobs permanently. Industry analysts estimate that the banks need to consolidate 20% more to be efficient. That translates to an additional 400,000 jobs lost. We tend to forget or underestimate the ripple effect of job cuts. In the case of the banks, surpluses of empty buildings will negatively impact the glutted commercial real estate markets. Reductions in the work forces of those who service banks such as building maintenance, advertising, accounting, law, information, restaurant, and office supplies are inevitable and should be expected.

The airline industry in the United States is also shrinking. The good news is that the four or five carriers left will allow the United States to compete with the giant state-run foreign airlines for global market share. But the bad news is that airline fares are likely to rise or at least not come down, making it more expensive for cash-strapped businesses to survive. If the airlines such as TWA that are in bankruptcy or default eventually fail, the loss of jobs and the ripple effect will further speed the coming depression.

FAULT LINE 3:
The End of Investment

Alas, there is a more frightening fault line, one that rarely makes the headlines and thus is ignored by the general public: the lack of investment by businesses. During the 1980s the Japanese invested 25% of their national output into new plants. The Japanese expect growth. And because they're optimistic about the future, Japanese companies keep building and upgrading production, which will keep many industries busy even through the recession. What have U.S. manufacturers done? More concerned about short-term profits than long-term financial health, they have actually cut capital investment as they sense the stormy weather ahead.

Moreover, it's not just capital investment which suffers from management neglect. For all their rhetoric about wanting skilled workers, U.S. corporations as a whole have followed a policy of not investing in their work forces. Adjusted for inflation, the amount spent on training has actually dropped over the 1980s. And the public sector has not made up the gap. Where West Germany spends 1% of its national output on public employment and training programs, the United States spends only one-third as much. This is not the behavior of an economy which expects to grow and needs skilled workers. Instead, it's the mark of a society in decline.

Of course, the U.S. companies that want to invest are laboring under a real constraint: lack of money. Profits in the 1980s were feeble, and much of corporate America put itself into deep debt as part of the merger and takeover boom. Retailing giant R. H. Macy paying interest on $6 billion it borrowed not for new stores but simply to "go private" was forced to seek bankruptcy protection.

To prevent a hostile takeover in 1988, USG Corp., the nation's largest wallboard maker raised debt to $2.6 billion, paying yearly interest as high as 16%. When the real estate market fell apart, this back-breaking debt almost forced the company to seek bankruptcy protection.

Famed architect and developer John C. Portman like many other developers was also forced into a credit squeeze when real estate floundered. Portman couldn't service a staggering $2.1 billion debt as vacancies rose in his many properties worldwide.

Moreover, companies have gotten locked into expenses that contribute little to productivity. Take the health care system, for example. Expenditures have risen at an annual rate of more than 10% in the 1980s, far outpacing inflation. Now health care takes about 10% of GNP, up from 8% in 1975. And much of the increase has been going for administrative costs, as companies try to control their health care expenditures. What's even worse, the high cost of health care is making labor more expensive, which causes companies to cut jobs even more.

Of course, there was one type of investment which did boom in the 1980s. That's computers, which took the lion's share of business investment spending. Sometimes it seems that that's all companies spent on—computers and office buildings.

But, now, the investment in computers has turned into a source of stress on the economy. The only way to make these big investments in information processing pay off is to use computers to replace people, and that's what companies are doing now. All across the economy, companies are laying off workers and using computers so that one worker can do the jobs five were doing before. The best example is Wall Street, which can now handle four times as many trades with fewer back office workers. The same goes for insurance companies.

If the economy were growing, these cutbacks would be beneficial rather than harmful. Productivity would rise, and laid-off workers would just find other jobs, either in the same company or in another one. But in a nogrowth environment, the replaced workers merely move to the unemployment line, and frightened consumers cut back spending.

FAULT LINE 4:
The Breakdown of the Early Warning Signs

This may be the most crucial fault line, because it's the one thing the "experts" don't understand. *We have added*

the element of surprise to the depression scenario. Since
our top economists, politicians, and businesspeople still
don't believe that a depression is inevitable and won't
take appropriate action, the depression will last far
longer and be deeper and more painful than if we had
prepared for it.

Why are the "experts" still blinded? Since the 1970s
there have been two distinct forces working simultaneously to shape our economy. The experts mistakenly
viewed these two forces as one. Let's explore their logic
trap.

Most economists and business forecasters believe in
what is called "the business cycle" and in the ability of
monetary policy to control its effects. They view this current recession as a natural and expected event as part of
the boom-and-bust pattern of U.S. economic activity for
more than a century.

First, comes an expansion phase usually lasting
three to four years. This phase is believed to start when
interest rates and inflation are low, which is where the
economy is now. At this point, the "experts" would expect consumers to borrow money and make purchases of
big ticket items such as cars, homes, furniture, and appliances. Corporations, predicting increased consumer
demand and greater profits, borrow money to increase
production to meet anticipated heightened consumer demand. Institutional and individual investors buy stocks,
anticipating corporate profits. The service and high-tech
sectors typically expand as the manufacturing sector requires more of their products and services.

As demand for credit increases and more borrowers
compete for loans, interest rates start to rise. Inflation
increases as the rising demand for goods and services
sparks price and wage increases. A decline in spending
occurs as tightened credit cuts back demand for the
more expensive products. This decline is a signal that
the contraction phase in the business cycle is underway.

Factories and the service sector cut back production and lower prices to move inventory. Consumer and business borrowing declines. Investors sell stock, anticipating lower corporate profits. Layoffs increase, and consumer spending decreases. At this point, we are in a recession. The government, under pressure to stimulate economic activity, agrees to print new money and let it "trickle down into the economy." But this, as Paul Tsongas correctly described it, is like "giving the horses oats to feed the birds."

The hard truth is that the type of problems that will be facing U.S. industry cannot be solved by monetary policy or reliance on an automatic self-correcting "business cycle rebound."

The fault lines of international failure and the stagnation and consolidation of the manufacturing, service, and high-tech sectors have created situations that are not of a cyclical nature but are structural. The economy isn't "simply weak" or sick. It has been stricken with profound, fundamental internal problems that no amount of economic pump-priming by the Fed can ever cure. The recent massive layoffs aren't temporary, they're jobs permanently lost. Foreign ownership of U.S. business is virtually irreversible. The record number of bank failures and bankruptcies have dug economic holes that no "upturn" can ever fill in. The list of economic woes is a long one: intense global competition, record welfare rolls, insane government regulations, global overcapacity, unbridled consumer debt, stagnating incomes, declining education levels, and increased crime. These issues will paralyze our economic, social, and political environment for years to come.

NO BOUNCEBACK

The United States is no stranger to recessions. Since the end of World War II, the country has lived through eight downturns. Some, like the one of 1969–70, were merely gentle pauses in growth. Others, like the recession of 1981–82, devastated the Midwest and much of the manufacturing sector. But always before, a combination of government policy and the natural vitality of the U.S. economy has brought a strong end to the downturn.

Unfortunately, that's not going to bail us out next time. Taken together, the econoquake's four fault lines are undercutting the economy, driving it into a downward spiral that won't be easy to escape. Indeed, the U.S. economic structure now bears a disturbing resemblance to a bucket with a lot of little holes at the bottom. The holes have been getting bigger for years, and it's going to be very hard to plug them all. Indeed, there are so many holes at the bottom of the bucket that the only thing left to do is to throw the bucket away and start again—and this is a far more radical step than most people are willing to contemplate. (See Chapter 10.)

THE GLOBAL
EMPLOYMENT BUST
OF THE 1990s

We go downhill very fast over here. The full impact
of the depression is just beginning to be felt. Until
lately, thousands of people were able to get along on
their savings, but now their savings begin to vanish
. . . . The cities are going broke one by one . . . . The
industrials have all gone to hell. For the first time in
my life I begin to give serious thought to money; it is
a new experience for me . . . . I hope to
continue to eat.

H. L. Mencken

"Brother, can you spare a dime?"

Popular song in the 1930s[1]

Just as there are earthquakes that hit with a potent
force exceeding 7 on the Richter scale, there are also frequent little quakes or tremors that signal the existence
of problems deep within the earth. In time, the power of
these forces reaches the point where the earth's sub-

structure can no longer contain them, and a major earth-quake results.

We are at such a point today in our economy. The signals, the "little tremors," are all around us. The meaning of these signals is clear when they are properly related, but most of us can't as yet comprehend the inevitable consequences that the tremors foretell. It's simply too scary. In this chapter we take a helicopter view of our economic puzzle to study the pieces and to see the unmistakable picture when the pieces come together. Announcements of plant closings have become a standard feature of the news in the United States in spite of the fact that the national media report only the largest ones. The rise in the jobless rate is at its highest in eight years. Unemployment statistics are also regular news fare, but as bad as the network anchors make them sound, they are really much worse. That's because the definition of un-employed includes only people actively looking for jobs. The number of people without jobs longer than 26 weeks has doubled since 1960, and current unemployment has been steadily climbing. Since 1988, one quarter of those unemployed have been without work for more than six months. *In Chapter 9, I make recommendations regarding jobs and education.*

We are more aware of plant closings and layoffs now because the United States is experiencing a recession that has lasted longer and is deeper than the experts predicted. These closing and layoffs are the "little tremors" from the fault lines we talked about in the last chapter. They are emblematic of the continuous shrinking of U.S. industry that has been going on since the 1970s.

WHY ANYBODY LAID OFF TODAY WILL HAVE TROUBLE FINDING A COMPARABLE JOB

Between 1969 and 1976, plant closings eliminated an estimated 15 million jobs, for an average of nearly 1.9 million jobs per year. Jobs in the manufacturing sector have been steadily declining. Indeed, even in the period 1979–1989, when overall employment increased more than 18 million, the manufacturing sector had a net loss of 1.4 million jobs.

Among the industries that have been experiencing declining employment are three important basics: transportation, steel, and tires. And the trend isn't likely to improve soon. The Big Three automakers are in trouble, and Chrysler has fallen out of the top three as Japan's Honda Motor Company overtakes it as a producer of U.S. cars. Chrysler is under enormous financial pressure just as it confronts a critical five-year, $15 billion product development plan. After five years of phenomenal growth, Chrysler's minivans—representing one out of five vehicles sold and more than 50% of the operating profits—and its Jeep brands are not selling so well. *In 1990, Chrysler cut $1.5 billion in future savings.*

And while some laid-off autoworkers were able to find new full-time jobs in other industries, their compensation was slashed. Not only did they earn an average of 30% less than they did in the auto industry, but 41% no longer had any employer-paid health insurance, 56% had no employer-paid pension, and 40% had no employer-paid life insurance.

The Peace Dividend

The prospect of military base closings highlight how connected the U.S. economy is with the government sector. Indeed, adjusting to the decline in defense spending may be the hardest part of the recession for California. McDonnell Douglas Corporation, a defense contractor employing 130,000 people, made the largest one-day layoff in corporate history when it gave termination notices to 1,700 employees on July 16, 1990. GE Aerospace, under pressure to boost profits and improve its ability to compete for new business, will eliminate about 2,000 jobs by the end of 1992. This comes on top of a 2,000-person cut in 1991.

The Service Sector

As companies cope with shrinking defense procurements and budgets, the commercial sector is no longer able to absorb laid-off workers as it did in the 1980s. Between December 1982 and July 1984, almost as many jobs were created in the wholesale and retail trade industry as in all durable manufacturing industries put together. McDonald's hamburgers, the bulk of whose employees earn little more than minimum wage, actually became a larger employer than U.S. Steel!

Retailing, one of the largest commercial (service) sector employers, has also been hard hit. Between September 1990 and the end of December 1990, there was a loss of about 150,000 jobs in the retail field, and current evidence strongly indicates a continuation of the trend. The recession is partly the blame, but fierce competition and heavy corporate debt loads have also pressured companies to cut back.

THE DECLINE IN THE NUMBER OF MANAGERIAL AND PROFESSIONAL JOBS

But job loss isn't limited to manufacturing and blue-collar positions. It is happening across the whole range of our industrial elite. The number of people employed by our largest industrial companies decreased by more than 20% between 1979 and 1989. Our top companies eliminated 3.7 million jobs in that ten-year period.

As companies face cutbacks, a growing number of professionals, managers, and clerical support workers are joining the ranks of the unemployed. The news media have portrayed this recession as particularly difficult for white-collar workers, not because of their numbers alone, but because many of them find it virtually impossible to gain comparable employment. As of February 1991, white-collar workers accounted for 32.7% of the 8.16 million unemployed, compared with 44.3% from three blue-collar groups and 21.2% from service occupations.

The belief that the current and future contraction will be harder on white-collar workers is based on the recent increases in the percentage of white-collar unemployed. Since August 1989, the number of unemployed workers has jumped by 485,000, of which the great majority—65%—are managers, professionals, and clerical workers. *A survey of 1,000 companies showed that 86% of the companies surveyed reduced their managerial ranks in the past five years; 52% reduced them in 1990.* And, with the exception of construction workers, the blue-collar unemployment rate has scarcely risen over the past year; many factory workers lost their jobs in the 1980s, leaving fewer to eliminate now.

Although the overall economic impact of white-collar layoffs has been lessened by generous severance and early retirement packages, these payments are decreasing. Once they run out, the economic impact could be devastating. Cutbacks are not limited to a single part of the economy; they are in all industries, and more white-collar layoffs seem inevitable.

The banking and financial services industries are especially vulnerable. Since the October 1987 stock market crash, 75,000 people in New York's banking and financial service sectors have lost their jobs. Some laid-off white-collar workers are settling for part-time work. A growing number of information systems workers who have been left jobless because of the shrinking economy have turned to contract labor while conducting a search for long-term work.

Even the advertising industry is feeling the pinch. With the recession looming on the heels of industry mergers and acquisitions, reduced client spending will get worse. Middle management agency executives and veteran creative talent with salaries well over six figures are often the first target for cost cutters. Few of this group are likely to apply for welfare checks soon; however, because of their previous high compensation, they will have problems finding equivalent positions. Many creatives have instead turned to freelancing, while unemployed managers join a growing army of independent consultants.

THE FALL IN MIDDLE CLASS LIVING STANDARDS

As companies reduce their work forces, the cuts are frequently deepest in middle management. These managers, sales executives, bankers, accountants, data processing executives, along with their skilled blue-collar neighbors were once the solid foundation of middle class America. In the 1970s, buying houses and condos and raising families in the suburbs while putting money away for their retirement and the kids' education was the American dream. In all its individualized forms, the dream has been the lure that has brought young people into our companies to start careers and has attracted immigrants to start new lives.

As the industrial consolidation and fierce international competition compel corporations to cut whole layers of management, negative shock waves affect us and our once secure environment. No longer are the big companies going to be the providers of paychecks, pensions, and health insurance. Many of us feel alone and abandoned.

THE PSYCHOLOGY OF UNEMPLOYMENT

Unemployment, however, is not statistics; it is people. For the newly unemployed, the stages of mourning are not dissimilar to other tragic events in life, like serious illness and death. The people who can bounce back quickest are those who can express their anger and who immediately move on to the next phase in life. I learned the damaging effects of structural unemployment on workers by interviewing over 100 workers who had been laid-off when the Brooklyn Navy Yard was closed in the late 1960s. Among my observations was the longer people are unemployed, the less likely they will find jobs on their own. The long-term unemployed lose faith in the unions, government, family, and friends and eventually become deeply gripped by despair. They also lose the ability to plan and, in spite of having little income, make large-ticket purchases they can't afford. Today the sheer number of the unemployed lessens the guilt and makes recovery somewhat easier. And as women's participation in the labor force has become more common and permanent, spousal earnings operate as a safety net when men lose jobs and vice versa.

Even the still-employed are wounded. Trust deteriorates and suspicion abounds among employees who remain after layoff.

Two groups suffer most when jobs are slashed. Companies typically target older workers for layoff and retirement. Blacks and Hispanics also experience a disproportionately heavy share of unemployment in recessionary periods, and during hard times, the proportion of blacks and Hispanics being reemployed as compared to whites is quite low. These groups are increasingly going to court with the Equal Employment Opportunity Commission when bias in layoffs or firings is alleged.

WHY THE U.S. NO LONGER HAS A COMPETITIVE ADVANTAGE IN SKILLED LABOR

In December 1980 in Taiwan, as I met with a group of bright, young, information-hungry Taiwanese, I sensed they were ready for their assigned task. As part of a Stanford Research Institute (SRI) team, I worked with a

Taiwanese task force in the 1980s to develop an information industry strategic plan for the People's Republic of China. The plan included a national commitment to train large numbers of Taiwanese students in computer-related technical courses.

The plan was similar to one I worked on earlier for the government of Singapore. Both countries were intent on developing policies and programs that moved their countries away from being sources of low-end, high-volume labor, which consisted primarily of intensive parts assembly work for Japanese, American, and European companies who could no longer afford to do similar work in their own countries. Singapore, Taiwan, Hong Kong, and the Republic of Korea remember that it was not that long ago that the Japanese were the makers of cheap, low-end products for U.S. manufacturers. These countries, known as the Little Dragons, decided to go after the value-added high-tech markets where the profits stayed in the country rather than flowing into the pockets of offshore companies. Because their industries are politically controlled, these countries are able to dictate the direction in which they want their economies to go.

With a wealth of skilled high-tech workers, the Acer Group changed from a small Taiwanese computer operation into a multinational high-technology conglomerate within a remarkably short time. Today, Acer is Taiwan's largest computer company, and Taiwan is the world's sixth largest producer of information products. Acer Group has reached $1 billion in revenue and is expanding its complex so that it can produce 1.2 million personal computers (PCs) this year. It has teamed up with Texas Instruments to build a $250 million memory chip plant. It has also bought a struggling California company called Altos that makes very powerful desktop computers called workstations.

In the early 1980s, IBM personal computers were bought not only because of IBM's reputation for technical innovation, reliability, and service, but also because there were no competitors offering similar products. Today, IBM is 1 of 300 producers of IBM-compatible PCs. Not only have many of these competitors edged aside IBM's reputation for technical innovation, but they also developed better reputations for reliability with such services as quick on-site repair at no additional cost.

Acer initially focused on imitations, emphasizing value. Today, however, it places increased emphasis on research and development (R&D), which has led to the development of the first Chinese language software.

U.S. companies in high tech and manufacturing, pressured by declining sales and profits, are shifting production to foreign countries. GM, Ford, and Chrysler are building cars in Mexico where workers earn $10 to $20 a day. With labor that cheap, the Big Three don't have to buy expensive capital equipment such as robotics to compete with 20 other car producers. (And, remember, less than 15 years ago there were only three or four players in the U.S. auto industry.)

GLOBAL PROBLEM

The Big Three U.S. automakers and foreign companies like Acer, however, are suffering as markets as diverse as personal computing and autos remain soft in North America and Europe. Indeed, unemployment is fast becoming a global problem. After five years of sustained job creation between 1985 and 1990, unemployment in Europe has started to rise since the latter half of 1990. European companies are suddenly cutting employees at a furious pace. Over 900,000 Europeans have lost their jobs between 1990 and midyear 1991, most in 1991. Currently there are 12.5 million people unemployed, for an official rate of 8.7%.

As Europe's downturn continues into this year, the jobless toll in France is now at an all-time high, and unemployment in the United Kingdom is heading up to the disastrous levels of the mid-1980s. Though the slowdown is relatively mild except in the United Kingdom, corporations are making deeper cuts than in past recessions. Defense, automobiles, textiles, leather, and clothing industries will have particular problems. Also as the single European market becomes a reality, many fear increased competition, especially from the Japanese. The trends are troublesome: unemployment is predicted to rise to 9.2% by the end of 1992; youth unemployment is twice the adult rate, and female unemployment twice that of males.

Also, the former Soviet bloc countries are facing rising unemployment due to worsened economic conditions, and long-term joblessness is becoming prevalent. Unified Germany had been the exception. Thanks to an infusion of DM 140 billion from government and the private sector to aid reunification, Germany has added 700,000 jobs during the 1990–91 period. But of late Germany's economy is beginning to slide.

Current Layoffs to Squash Any Incipient Recovery

The number of U.S. job cuts already announced, which are going to take place during the next few years will kill any chance for a long-lived recovery. GM's planned layoff of 74,000 is yet to happen. Digital Equipment Corp. (DEC) announced a 2,000-employee cutback, but this is only the first installment of an anticipated 16,000 jobs to be cut by 1993. Unisys has a grim forecast for the future: 10,000 employees who will lose their jobs. With the Bank of America and Security Pacific merger, another 10,000 jobs may be lost. Allied-Signal and Time-Warner are just a few of the many other large companies who have announced layoffs.

Ripple Effect of Job Cuts

Most of these reductions are permanent and not cyclical adjustments. These jobs are gone! What's worse, every corporate job cut costs at least one more job in the rest of the economy. The economy is unraveling like a wound-up ball of rubber bands, as scared consumers stop spending and businesses fire even more people to stay afloat. Many small business companies with fewer than 100 employees are sinking. These businesses make up 98% of the failed businesses. And the survivors are running scared and not borrowing for capital expenditures.

Think of how vulnerable the economy is now, and then imagine a series of massive layoffs hitting the economy like tidal waves hitting an unprotected beach. As each wave hits, it erodes consumer confidence, and people perceive that there are not enough jobs available for them to feel secure about spending money on either luxuries or basics. As people use savings to pay home, food, car, utility, and insurance bills, they have less discretionary income at the end of the month. This means a necessary downsizing in spending patterns for the 1990s.

States and Cities Are Hurting

Layoffs and slower business activity keep rippling through states' economies, thus eroding tax collections. Simultaneously, the jobless are turning to the states for unemployment and welfare programs, boosting state spending. Deficits and pressure to cut more state and local government jobs are the result. The groups that are pressuring state and local governments to cut their payrolls often don't realize how dependent their local economies are on government payrolls. On Long Island, New York, 10% of the employment base is deriving an income from schools, but with a $689 million budget gap looming in New York State, there is great pressure on the school budget. Meanwhile, Florida is projecting a $622 million shortfall after just cutting $1 billion.

The nation's cities are facing both large budget deficits and unhappy choices. If they raise taxes on commercial property, they risk driving out businesses and jobs. If they cut spending and reduce services to balance budgets, they make the city a less desirable place to work and live. In most of the nation's cities, "for sale" and "for rent" signs are proliferating quietly like wire hangers in dark closets.

WHAT THIS DEPRESSION WILL BE LIKE

Depression. It's a word that strikes fear in most of us, conjuring up images of cold, hungry men on long breadlines, apple peddlers on street corners, farm foreclosures, and swollen relief roles. But it is alien to most of us because only our oldest remember the Great Depression of the 1930s. Recession, on the other hand, is an experience we are quite familiar with. It's a word the economists use when the gross national product (GNP), the total value of goods and services produced in the United States, declines for two consecutive quarters and is considered a natural and expected part of what economists call the business cycle (see Chapter 5). We've had eight recessions since the end of World War II, and they lasted on the average only about a year. As we wait for this expected upturn, we hear the "R" word nightly on the evening news.

During the econoquake depression, most people's standard of living will spiral downward as falling sales lead to less employment. Real income determines material living standards and is the best measure of economic progress. A depression interrupts progress, so if real income stops growing, it is reasonable to regard the economy in a depressed state. If you look at the measures of real income for the worker and the family, you can only conclude that the economy has been in a depressed state since 1973. Since 1973, weekly earning declined at an annual rate of 1.22%. (The reasons for this subsurface silent decline are discussed in Chapter 4.)

The severity of the depression is dependent on how people, business, and particularly government react during the early stages.

The Best Case Scenario

Consider a two- to three-year depression followed by a strong sustained recovery without inflation. Under this scenario, the government will quickly recognize that this depression is not going to go away by itself, that it's a structural problem that will prevent any upswing in the business cycle, and that the monetary policies of the Federal Reserve will not bring an end to the downturn. So the government implements massive spending to keep the economy afloat, while beginning the restructuring policies as outlined in Chapter 10.

Unfortunately, this case is unlikely, since politicians and economists have not yet accepted that they have a serious problem which requires extraordinary treatment. Like the alcoholic who doesn't admit he is one and thus cannot seek help, this dissonance between perception and reality can delay the onset of recovery for years.

The Worst Case Scenario

Consider a severe long-term (six to eight years') depression coupled with social unrest. A state of national emergency is declared, giving authoritarian control to the president. There is rising crime as instigators provoke looting. Bankrupt state and city governments are forced to curtail services as tax revenues fall. In this scenario, it was politics as usual, Washington providing lip service only, while waiting for the upturn in the business cycle that always seems to be another six months away. Proposed economic and social long-range planning was dismissed as an interference with free market system.

The fragile economic support and protection safety nets built to handle a modest percentage of the population are tattered as greatly increased needs arise from all segments of the population.

The Guarantees Are Gone. Social security, welfare, food stamps, unemployment, Medicare, child care, and other benefit programs that were already collapsing in good times will be overwhelmed, exhausted, or severely curtailed by this scenario. And the Federal Deposit Insurance Corporation (FDIC), whose function is to stop you from withdrawing money when you are worried, will not be able to reimburse you in the event of a nationwide banking crisis. Although the sticker of government deposit insurance on your bank's front door is reassuring, the resources behind it are virtually nonexistent. The reserve fund to pay off depositors when a bank fails currently equals about 1% of the deposits it is meant to cover. The predicted collapse of 75% of the nation's banks under this scenario overwhelms the system.

The early phase resembles the Ayn Rand world where the takers keep expecting more from the doers. *This makes it impossible to restart the economic engines of growth.* Remember, a large percentage of the country is already getting some form of government assistance. As business failures increase and the numbers of the unemployed increase, a true capitalist underground economy, where people sell products and services off the books, flourishes, while the government bureaucrats are given control of emergency rationing of food and other resources. Of course, payoffs and corruption are standard operating procedure. Interestingly, the economy has some resemblance to what is happening in the former Soviet Union today.

The Most Likely Case

Consider a long-term (three to six years') depression with recovery taking most of the decade. The early stages will be deflationary as the Federal Reserve System pulls out all stops in an unsuccessful attempt to bring about a recovery. Interest rates are kept low, and the government reduces taxes for the middle class. The federal debt ceiling will keep rising as spending increases while tax revenues fall. Business failures will rise dramatically.

Health benefits will be made available to all, but only basic health needs will be covered, under a model similar to the one developed by an interdisciplinary task force in Oregon. Social security will be prorated based on financial need. Special low-interest loans will be made available to business. The Federal Housing Authority (FHA) will increase the availability of federal mortgage money, and further tax incentives will be initiated to make home ownership more affordable while keeping the building trades working. Foreclosures will increase, however, as people will not be able to make mortgage payments. Cash will become the payment of choice, and the underground economy will flourish.

A new jobs program is developed to employ the millions who have lost jobs. The program works to provide shelter for the growing homeless population, run massive food kitchens, rebuild city infrastructures, maintain parks, and perform environmental cleanup projects. Unemployment benefits are extended for a year as unemployment rises to levels unknown since the 1930s. Massive training grants are authorized to retrain workers. Many people relocate to areas where the living costs are more affordable such as the Ozarks. There is public desire for price supports, protectionism, and a large decrease in defense spending. We can expect a deeply troubled economy at least until 1998 and perhaps through the early 2000s.

COMPARING THE 1930s AND THE 1990s

Nobody can predict exactly what this depression will be like, but it's a safe bet it won't be the same as the last one. However, some of the similarities and differences will provide a framework for understanding our current depression.

Beginnings

The 1930s. The 1930s Great Depression began with a strange stubborn recession and stock market crash. A recession in business was under way even before the stock market collapsed at the end of October 1929. Experience proved quite different from 1924 and 1927 when mild recessions had apparently been checked by the easing of credit. In fact, production slipped downward almost steadily until late in 1932 or early 1933, when about one-third of the nation's resources were standing idle. Thereafter, a somewhat halting recovery took place. The slump seems to have had a double bottom for a brief recovery in the fall of 1932, and was followed by a renewed decline in the first months of 1933. It was not until World War II that our resources were as fully employed as they had been in 1929.

The 1990s. The recessions we experienced in 1991 and 1992 can be compared with the recession of 1927, which was controlled by the easing of credit. A long-term recession will be underway before the second quarter of 1993, and this recession will be similar to the recession prior to the 1929 stock market crash. This recession will actually be the early phase of the econoquake.

Tax Collection

The 1930s. Prior to World War II, people paid income taxes during the year following the receipt of income, so in 1930 and 1932 people were paying taxes long after they lost their jobs.

The 1990s. Pay-as-you-go withholding by the employer now ensures that people stop paying taxes when their earnings cease. This helps maintain some consumer purchasing power when a recession starts.

Government Policy Making

The 1930s. As soon as it had become clear that the stock market boom had ended, the Federal Reserve eased credit. For example, the New York Reserve Bank's discount rate was reduced from the 6.5% it had been in November 1929 to 2.5% in June 1930 and further reduced to 1.5% in May 1931. This form of helpful encouragement to business makes for cheap and abundant credit. Easing of the money market had checked the recessions of 1924 and 1927. Why didn't it work in 1930? The Fed was criticized then for not acting early or vigorously enough after the 1929 stock market crash.

The 1990s. The Federal Reserve lowered interest rates to the lowest point in years to pump up a deflated economy. But as in the 30s, the Fed had been accused of not acting promptly to relax interest rates.

Unemployment Compensation

The 1930s. Month by month, unemployment rose to ever-higher levels. These were the days of breadlines, apple sellers, and swollen relief rolls. As scores of people competed for the same job, salaries were cut continually for those who retained jobs. Still, they counted themselves lucky. Honor graduates tried to sell silk stockings door to door to housewives who couldn't afford to buy them. Once wealthy families starved in their large unsalable homes, attended by loyal but unpaid servants.

The 1990s. The average person is eligible for 26 weeks of unemployment compensation, which will be continually extended to avoid economic collapse. The small business owner cannot take advantage of the over-supply of labor to reduce wages because he must observe laws mandating a minimum wage. Of course, when personal earnings drop, so does social security tax collection, placing even greater strains on a fragile economy as it prepares for a growing aging population.

Banks

The 1930s. During the period 1931–32, almost 3,600 banks closed their doors, causing a loss of purchasing power as peoples' savings were wiped out and local businesses failed to obtain working capital. The failures of even a few unsound banks had led to the distrust of sound banks and to a widespread hoarding of currency. During the early months of 1933, public distrust of the banks became so great that the entire banking system had to be put on holiday while an emergency currency could be produced and legalized.

Hoarding of currency mounted rapidly in late 1932, and by March 4, 1933, New York banks, scared by heavy withdrawals, asked for a moratorium. President Roosevelt proclaimed a four-day bank holiday to begin March 6. Panic was averted and Congress was given a breather to pass The Emergency Banking Act of 1933, which enabled banks to open at the earliest possible date.

The 1990s. A loss of purchasing power owing to a wave of bank failures is unlikely since the federal government has underwritten losses from bank failures. The FDIC offers deposit insurance as its chief vehicle carrying out its mandate to maintain confidence in and provide stability to the commercial banking system. However, the FDIC is currently experiencing the highest level of bank failures since the Great Depression. Management and shareholders of banks, who are well aware that bank runs occur when depositors perceive banks to be insolvent, are finally monitoring their loan officers more closely to avoid undertaking risky investments.

Other Scary Similarities Between the 1930s and the 1990s

Both the 1930s and the 1990s have experienced record corporate bankruptcy, jittery financial markets, and eroding public confidence as individuals saw their savings and spending declining. In the 1990s, as in the 1930s, property markets worldwide are crashing, and the financial system is under great strain.

Today as then, there exist worldwide product surpluses. Today as then, we are moving from a period of high inflation to one of deflation. Both periods are characterized by a growing protectionist sentiment, declining population growth, and a dearth of new industries, which creates an environment of stagnating capital investment opportunities. Both periods are characterized by a government that discourages business, including excessive government regulation of business, a highly progressive taxation code, and policies that increase labor costs.

The images from the 1930s—the bread lines and soup kitchens, the educated apple sellers—though not experienced at first hand by most of us, haunt us still. In the 1990s, the images of unemployment may look different, yet for some of us, visions of becoming a "bag lady" or descending into homelessness, are visiting the outskirts of our consciousness. Among the subtle side effects of these premonitions is a wish to hold on to what we still have. Naturally, such an attitude is helping to create an exceedingly cool investment climate.

ENDNOTES

1. (E.Y. Harburg, Jay Garney) © 1932 Warner Bros.
    Inc. (Renewed). Rights for the extended renewal
    term in U.S. controlled by Glocca Morra Music and
    Gorney Music Publishers and administered by the
    Songwriters Guild of America. All rights for the
    work, excluding the U.S., controlled by Warner
    Bros. Inc. All Rights Reserved. Used by permission.

CHILLY INVESTMENT
CLIMATE OF THE 1990s

*There are opportunities for the lions when
the herd is confused.*

Barry Minkin

T hroughout this book I have used the earthquake
analogy to discuss the coming economic collapse. In reality, however, the physical world will not change much.
Bankrupt factories will close, but the buildings will still
be standing. The real estate market may collapse, but
there will still be row upon row of houses in neighbor-
hoods throughout the land.

The econoquake is primarily a financial catastro-
phe, and the financial collapse has yet to come. Even the
term *financial collapse* is misleading since real wealth
will still exist. What will change is the ownership. The
wealthy of tomorrow will be the people and institutions
of today who understand what is happening and who act
accordingly. A depression—and that is what the
econoquake most resembles—is a period of drastic financial decline and capital liquidation. That means, among
other things, that people who bought assets foolishly in

the 1980s will unload them at fire sale prices in an attempt to stave off financial ruin. That's precisely what happened to the Japanese company that bought Pebble Beach in California just a few years ago for over $800 million. At the time, people ranging from the average person in the street to the veteran analysts thought the purchase price was exorbitant. They were all correct. Realizing they overpaid, the Japanese firm unloaded the property in early 1992 for $500 million.

In this chapter I explore how the unfolding collapse will affect the investment climate of the 1990s. *There are many investment opportunities for those who quickly acclimate to the changing investment climate. Chapter 8 is a guide to effective investment strategies and opportunities in the 1990s.*

In much of the 1980s, investing was child's play. Stocks, junk bonds, and every other investment went up, and everyone knows a story about someone who made a killing on one type of investment or another. Big money was made by people who invested in real estate, government bonds, and stocks a decade ago. Equities gained so much value during the 1980s that even after the big crash of 1987, most people whose holdings were more than two years old still enjoyed a net gain.

Nineteen ninety-two is a peculiarly interesting time in history. The financial markets are an investor's dream, interest rates are way down, and inflation as measured by the consumer price index is at the lowest of any recession since 1970. At the same time, the stock market has rallied, mutual funds contain millions of new investor dollars, and the bond market has soared. The business climate should be outstanding because both the benchmark prime lending rate and oil prices are low. The good news should continue, according to John Naisbitt, the well-known futurist who is predicting a global economic boom for the 1990s. He is not alone in seeing a rosy future. *Businessweek* published similarly upbeat views in its fourth quarter 1992 predictions by 50 economists. The consensus: unemployment will be no higher than 6.8% by year's end, and fourth quarter GNP will be 2.2% above 1991 levels.

But although the experts expect the financial markets to build up momentum, the public is being much more cautious. The recession has lasted longer and is deeper than many experts had predicted, and investors see little cause for optimism in the primary economic indicators. Gross national product (GNP) has not grown faster than 1.9% in any quarter since 1989. Real income, suffering one of its deepest declines recorded in any postwar recession, will not firm up until jobs and wages improve, something that's not likely to happen soon.

Indeed, since 1973, median income has barely grown. Consumer spending is flat, and the almost daily announcements of new white-collar layoffs are making consumers very concerned about how much they spend. With record consumer debt and rapidly declining savings, most people just can't afford to buy. Normally, stagnation like this can be solved by government pump priming, and this time the easy-money policies of the Federal Reserve are trying to provide the hoped-for economic spark.

WHY THE 1990s WILL BE DISASTROUS FOR UNPREPARED INVESTORS

What makes these times perilous for investors is that they are having to make major financial decisions from confusing and sometimes even contradictory signals. The good news—low interest rates, low inflation rates, and low energy prices—are historically the factors that would provide the base on which to build an economic recovery. Yet consumer confidence remains at record lows, and companies shelve their expansion plans.

Unfortunately, the current rebound will be short lived. Indeed, the biggest mistake of both the advisors and their clients will be to continue to rely on the "natural and expected" nature of economic cycles and government policies to bring about a rebound (see Chapter 5). We are in a period of structural stagnation having little or nothing to do with cycles. These long-term structural problems such as the shrinking industrial base, an undercapitalized banking system, overbuilding in the commercial sector, declining worldwide markets, and fierce international competition are going to be the thermostats controlling our investment climate for the balance of the 1990s. And most economists and financial advisors—even doom-and-gloom writers, who predicted a Great Depression in 1990—are telling us that the future will be much like the past: recurring cycles of boom and bust. Hear it again: *the game has changed structurally.* If you are looking at past cycles to forecast future events, you will continually miss the mark. If you use past events to as a guide for future financial planning, you will suffer the severest of consequences during the 1990s.

As the recession deepens into a depression late in 1994, there will be an ever-increasing public outcry to do something about it. Both parties and growing political fringe groups will be lobbied by special interest groups to make sure they get a cut of the ever-shrinking pie. But don't expect the government to help, because it will be as economically depressed as any other major institutions.

Among the possible government "cures" to the depression are ever-extending unemployment benefits, giving handouts to riot-torn cites, making deeper interest cuts, cuting the capital gains tax, increasing the investment tax credit, expanding the individual retirement account (IRA) deduction, giving the middle class tax breaks, instituting wage and price controls, controlling bank account withdrawals, restricting imports and exports, restricting foreign ownership of businesses including nationalization, authorizing subsidies to endangered industries, regulating price supports, rationing, and even declaring a state of emergency. Unfortunately, as latter chapters will illustrate, none of these "cures" addresses the structural roots of the problem. They will just exacerbate a bad situation.

Indeed, our current administration has been faced with the choice of propping up the economy to give the impression that it is on the mend or allowing it to collapse in order for a restructuring to take place.

The thought of allowing increased unemployment and bankruptcy to cause a restructuring to take place is political suicide, so each administration does the politically expedient thing. They continue each year to play a shell game with the federal budget to forestall national foreclosure for another year and breathe a sigh of relief as they succeed in moving our problems into the future.

A traditional Keynesian response to a depression like this is to spend lots of money as a stimulus so that people can purchase excess inventories and get our factories moving. However, this time the problem is too much *debt*, not too much *inventory*. And if efforts to spur more consumption by massive government spending and making borrowing easier provide some short-term economic relief, they will soon lead to the pileup of even more debt, which will accelerate the decline. Since government is shooting in the dark at the wrong targets, the best we can hope for at this time is for the people in Washington to do as little as possible until a total government and industry restructuring plan can be developed.

THE INVESTMENT CLIMATE 1993–1998

Lane Kirkland, president of the AFL-CIO said, "Pappy told me never to . . . get into an argument with people

who buy ink by the barrel." It's my turn in the barrel.
Here's my forecast of the financial climate between the
fourth quarter 1993 and the fourth quarter 1998:

> Gross domestic product (GDP) growth will average
> less than 1% annually in the United States; manu-
> facturing will decline -0.3%; employment will de-
> cline -0.5%.

> Unemployment will reach double digits in 1994 and
> stay in double figures until a massive government
> work program is enacted.

> Inflation will be less than 5% through 1993 but
> steadily rising as the government needs to borrow
> massive amounts of cash to try to buy its way out of
> a depression.

> Food and energy costs will rise steadily, while hous-
> ing, clothing, and auto prices will drop.

This is how the financial scenario will play itself out:

Stage 1 (1993–Midyear 1994): Investor Confusion from Mixed Economic Signals

The proverbial lag of several months for the government
"cures" to spur the economy once again passes, and the
economists are once again surprised that we are quickly
in another stubborn recession. Despite some positive
signs, the recovery from a recession begun in late 1992
fails to take hold. Most significant is that the record
number of business failures continues. These failures,
combined with continued business consolidations
through mergers and acquisitions, are making for a
much smaller industrial base. While the administration
gloats over a "recovery," the patient is dying.

Layoffs continue unabated and real unemployment
moves over 10%, with the service sector and high tech
being hit hardest. Consumers are still addicted to shopping, but not for big-ticket goods. They spend their

money for escapism and make-me-feel-good items such as food and travel and not for new cars, furniture, and appliances.

A mild stock market crash happens in late 1992 or first quarter 1993, which brings to Dow below 3000, but the "Wall Street Week" optimists see it as just a healthy adjustment to the overheated market. Analysts recommend a gutsy stock buy since stocks are now available at marked-down prices. Energy prices remain low, but the Organization of Petroleum Exporting Countries (OPEC) is planning to meet to limit supply as world demand declines.

Stage 2 (Second half 1994–1996): Awareness That Most Asset Values Will Collapse in the 1990s

Most asset values are sustained by faith in the future, but as employment drops and the economy slows, more and more people lose that faith.

Company inventories are cut, but because sales decline even more steeply than expected, companies still hold bigger stockpiles than they want and can't use inflation as an excuse to raise prices. Falling income and savings cause panic as companies and individuals begin to sell their assets to secure cash. Inflated asset values are adjusted downward from 1980s levels, including gold, silver, diamonds, housing, art, and collectibles. Those individuals who buy assets wait like lions, watching the herds of wilderbeasts panic and run.

The stock market, which has been sustained by falling interest rates rather than earnings, continues to drop as people move money into government-secured funds and money market accounts.

Banks suffer enormous losses from real estate defaults and the inability to find credit-worthy customers, and businesses and individuals fail in record numbers. Most houses are now sold at foreclosure auctions at pre-1980 prices.

Business, already reeling, goes into a nosedive as sales decline and equity transfusions from the stock market slow to a trickle. There are a record number of bankruptcies each year, and auction sales of the assets of defunct businesses are well attended.

WHY THE HISTORICAL HIGH STOCK AVERAGES WON'T HOLD IN THIS DECADE

With the Dow Jones Industrial Average above 3,000, and with the profits people made in 1991, why aren't investors jubilant about 1992? Because they still remember the blows they took in the fall of 1987 and again in 1989 after the market blossomed to new highs in the summer of those years. They're asking if it is time to get out, while those on the sidelines are waiting for some signal to come in.

The signals say clearly, "Stay out," but this market has been marching to another drummer. It has been sustained by falling short-term interest rates rather than earnings increases. Indeed, with interest rates down, countless individuals and institutions are depending on the stock market to deliver the sort of performance that will enable them to reach their financial objectives. It's the best game in town. Although many stocks are overvalued, history has shown that long-term investors in common stocks fare better than investors in any other type of financial asset (see Chapter 8). Yes, equity investors are making money in this recession as the market continues bullish while I'm writing this book.

But money market managers are wary of the start of a bear market whenever the Dow Jones Industrial Average is near its all-time high. Indeed, the current multiples of book value, dividends, and earnings are at the highest reaches of historical valuation. It is illogical to presume that common stocks will prove immune to the econoquake forces while all other assets fail.

A rise in interest rates could be the red flag that sends the bull market out to pasture. Expect continued bad news as to bell wether companies, such as General Motors and IBM, continue to slip into ever-widening fault lines. As the need for cash increases, so do the anxiety levels. Expect the public to cash out and stay off the road rather than continue playing a dangerous game of chicken with a market not connected to economic reality. The longer investors flee from cashing out, the deeper the downturn in the market.

Prediction

The Dow will drop below 3000 *if interest rates rise* in second half 1992 or first quarter 1993. I would expect it to slide below 2650 in 1994. The wild card that could keep stocks at the 3000 level is the pension funds, which are nearing $6 trillion. About $4 trillion is private pension funds, which historically invest about half their funds in common stock. With only $2 trillion worth of stocks in the United States, the pension funds have more control on market direction than the earnings performance of the companies.

THE COMING WIPE-OUT OF RESIDENTIAL REAL ESTATE

As the song goes, "Those were the days my friend, we thought they'd never end."[1] But they have ended. For years, home owners swapped stories about $30,000 homes that were now worth $300,000 and more. In the Northeast and in California, home prices actually began falling sometime in 1990, and in most areas prices still have not bounced back.

Most areas experience the overheated market of the mid-1980s, when soaring prices had many of us believing that single-family homes were a good short-term investment. As people told tales of how much homes had appreciated, investors dropped out of stocks and bought houses.

The demographics were also historically positive in the 1980s. The huge baby-boom generation reached home-buying age and dramatically bid up home prices. The best investment in my Palo Alto, California, neighborhood, was selling houses that were doubling in value every few years. Parts of the Northeast were equally hot markets.

In the 1990s, the boomers have their houses, and the housing market growth is now dependent on the under-30 group, the "baby-bust" generation, which is losing the fight for prosperity. (See Chapter 6.) Current home owners have included the inflated value of their homes in their net worth spreadsheets and are counting on this money for their retirement. But now financially strapped families need to sell their homes. Unfortunately, demand is lower, in large measure because the younger generation cannot afford today's inflated prices. In many areas of California the inventory of unsold homes has tripled.

But the pressures of job loss or shortened work hours and a terrible business climate persist as do ever-increasing taxes, fees, insurance, and maintenance costs. Refinancing has helped those who are trying to stay put. But there is a leak in the dike—prices have begun to fall in many markets, including California where even during the 1981–82 recession, population growth kept prices rising.

However, now the buyers are slow to come into the market even with interest rates at their lowest in years. Indeed, 1991 was the worst year for housing starts since 1945. People see prices dropping and wonder how far they will fall. Others are waiting for a hinted further lowering of the rates. Increasingly buyers are turning to auctions and foreclosures for bargains, and with good reason. The foreclosures continue to grow.

Pundits will continue to point out that real estate is a good investment, since it increases at a greater rate than inflation and performs well in periods of high inflation when stocks and bonds do not. But to the growing number of middle class Americans struggling to keep a roof over their heads, discussions about inflation and buying a house as an investment are heard as echoes from a more prosperous past.

Prediction

The housing market will remain weak from second half of 1993 through 1998 because the economy is going to get weaker and demographic forces are negative toward housing. Inventories of unsold homes will increase in most areas nationally.

Foremost among the differences in local housing markets is the overall health and status of the local economy in the current environment. If the local economy is bad now, it will get worse. If it's been hit hard in past recessions, it will be hit hard again. And if it's doing well in this environment, prices will hold or fall more slowly and not go as deep. Homes with sale prices over $300,000 in California and the Northeast will be very difficult to sell, and prices will fall an average of 12% by the end of 1994.

More important, home values will no longer increase at a greater rate than inflation, as has always been the case—another example of how the historical relationships will not work in the econoquake. Commercial real estate investment will even be more dangerous, particularly in the Northeast. The South and West will continue to pull population from other areas.

THE BOND MARKET PROVIDES SOME GOOD NEWS FOR THE SHORT TERM

While recessions are bad for stocks, they are often good for bonds. Indeed, in the 1981–82 recession, long-term

Treasuries and investment-grade bonds earned a 44% return compared to 10% for stocks. This recession has been positive for bonds as well. Lehman Brothers, Inc.'s T-bond index, which measures price appreciation and interest income, was up 12% in 1991.

With inflation low and the Federal Reserve trying to jump start the economy by keeping interest rates down, the big winner should be the very-highest-grade bonds. A safe investment are Treasuries, backed by the full faith and credit of the U.S. government. Want to do better than Treasuries and still minimize risk, consider mortgage-backed securities, which are created by pooling home owners' notes. Government National Mortgage Association (GNMA) bonds, known as Ginnie Maes, deliver a coupon and the added benefit of a federal guarantee. There is one risk that the underlying mortgages can be repaid early as home owners' refinance at lower rates, forcing the issuer to call the bond.

Tax-exempt municipal bonds (munis) are becoming an even more attractive tax shelter as cash-strapped states introduce or raise personal income taxes. The depression, however, will make it difficult for many issuers of munis. Many state and local governments have been struggling with budget deficits for years but when Bridgeport, Connecticut, filed for bankruptcy protection, the nation took notice. Now, many localities are unable to repay their debts; indeed, there was $4.5 billion worth of muni defaults in 1991. As the downward trend in the economy and employment continues, there will be the additional fiscal stress fractures in the nation's cities and states. Buying bonds insured by AAA-rated insurance companies that make payments of interest and principal if an issuer defaults are a way to reduce risk. The infamous corporate junk bonds that bankrupted Drexel Burnham Lambert and got Michael Milken a prison cell had a great 1991. The market's total return rebounded an amazing 42%. These large returns were mostly a reaction to a bad 1990, when the average junk bond mutual fund dropped 11%. Individual investors looking for better yields and sensing the market had bottomed out put money back into the severely undervalued market. Yields in 1992 are expected to run about 10–11%. This market is very sensitive to public sentiment, and when the public is spooked, they will leave the market as happened in 1990. Also, at that time regulators forced insurance companies and thrifts to unload junk portfolios. As additional corporate bankruptcies scare away the public, there will be some opportunities for high risk takers who carefully select companies that are able to survive a depression such as the food and health industries.

Prediction

Many of the muni and junk issues will mature during this period, and companies and municipalities will have to refinance the bonds or pay out cash for them. Given the economic and investment climate, many will not be able to raise the money to meet their obligations. Prices of healthy issues will be dragged down by the bad news regarding defaults.

HOW THE PROBLEMS AT EVEN THE STRONGEST INSURANCE COMPANIES AND PENSION FUNDS WILL HIT RETIREES

As noted in *Businessweek,* "Americans, who spend about 5% of their disposable income on life insurance, trusted that their policies were grounded in a bedrock of solid investments. And with $1.4 trillion in assets, the U.S. insurance industry appeared well equipped to keep on delivering." That is, until the early econoquake shock wave began being felt. "Along came the collapse of Exec-

utive Life, First Capital, and Monarch, whose foundations were built on crumbling junk bonds and real estate
investments . . . . Mutual Benefit Life, with over $13 bil-
lion in assets, became the largest insurance failure in
history."

Shocked policyholders were left confused about
what would become of their benefits seized by state regulators. They won't be worrying alone. Over 15 million
annuityholders are counting on their insurance companies to provide them retirement benefits.

There are three basic types of employee pension
plans:

1. Defined benefit plans (DBP)

2. Defined contribution plan (DCP)

3. 401(k) plans

An employee in a DCP or a 401(k) is not promised a
specific benefit at retirement. The employer's obligations
to DCP and 401(k) are fulfilled on a current basis, as required contributions are made. If a DCP or 401(k) termi-
nates, the employer has no further obligations, whereas
an employer who adopts a DBP accepts an unknown cost
commitment. The Pension Benefits Guaranty Corp
(PBGC) insures a limited amount of benefits promised
by the DBP, but does not insure DCPs.

Unfortunately for U.S. workers, an increasing number of employers are terminating DBP's and replacing
them with uninsured DCPs. Unless major legislative reforms are enacted that deal with the myriad problems
facing the PBGC, increasing numbers of DBPs will ter-
minate.

Businessweek reports, there are the millions of people who invested in insurance-run products known as
guaranteed investment contracts (GICs), through their
company-sponsored 401(k) or other pension plans . . . .
About 65% of the money in such retirement plans is

parked in GICs . . . [which] resembles a certificate of deposit, since its principal value doesn't fluctuate and it pays a stated interest rate. But unlike other pension plans, GICs aren't federally insured: The money is usually only as good as the credit of the insurance company.

The sponsor of most pension plans including 401(k) does assume fiduciary responsibility for the way the funds are managed. "When Executive Life fell, the fate of the GIC-subscribing employees was in their employers' hands. Ralston Purina made its employees' investments whole . . . . Unfortunately for their employees, Honeywell and Unisys aren't paying."

Upset employees are suing both companies. Employees can sue the fund trustee if the pension funds dwindle, and the courts can force owners to forfeit their own retirement benefits to compensate employees for their losses.

Moreover, with states and cities facing budget deficits, politicians are trying to use some of the $878 billion set aside to pay the pensions of retired public employees for other purposes. In the past two years, more than one-third of the states have cut or delayed contributions to their pension funds, seized money outright from pension accounts, or begun to debate similar measures. In the private sector, massive job reductions, exemplified by General Motors planned elimination of 74,000 jobs, are eroding cash reserves of the pension funds of affected companies. Some companies are liquidating stock to pay pension benefits. (Unisys Corp., U.S. West, Inc., and Southwestern Bell had to liquidate pension assets to meet lump-sum distribution requests.)

Prediction

The insurance industry will not collapse as the banks did in the 1930s or the Savings and Loan associations (S&Ls) are doing now, mainly because most insurers are conservative, keeping half their portfolios in government or investment-grade bonds. But, like the banking industry, insurance regulators have a dismal record of identifying troubled companies early enough to stop the leaks. The pension funds of many U.S. workers will remain in jeopardy as commercial real estate investments and mortgage loans will bring continued bad news about insurance company failures.

HOW THE LOSS OF WEALTH WILL DAMPEN CONSUMER SPENDING

The 1980s was a decade of economic confidence and robust consumer spending. Personal consumption spending rose by $656 billion between 1980 and 1989, compared with $508 billion in the previous decade. The consumption frenzy was propelled by baby boomers setting up households, rapid increases in the value of housing, federal tax reductions, and the borrowing boom.

But, the 1990s will be different. The decade is likely to be characterized by eroding consumer confidence, depression, repayment of debts, and retirement. As the economy continues to sputter, a paralyzing fear that decreases consumer spending has already taken hold. Consumers feel in their guts that things are going to get worse in spite of constant talk by economists that prosperity is just around the corner. The consumers' mood is very important since consumer lending normally leads to economic recovery and consumer spending counts for two-thirds of GDP.

To be sure, businesses will have to see consumer spending improve before they add workers or move ahead with any new investments or capital projects. Consumers are most concerned about jobs which are difficult to find. After an extended period of relatively high unemployment, the finances of an increasingly large number of households have been adversely affected.

Over a recent 12-month period, about one in five households experienced a reduction in the income flow for an average of 5 to 6 months. And, in one-fourth or more of all instances, the jobless episode lasted 10 months or more. True, some of the financial loss of being without a paycheck for a long spell is offset by unemployment benefits. However, the damage can equate to as much as one-fourth or more of the total annual earnings.

In this area the squeezed middle class consumer will deplete his or her assets to survive the continuing economic assault. Consumers have dipped into savings rather than take on new debt. Personal savings fell sharply and is currently running well below the 4.6% norm. Interest income, contrary to popular belief, is earned primarily by those with moderate incomes rather than the rich. Those with incomes of less than $40,000 receive more than 50% of interest income earned in this country. Those moderate-income people who count on interest income are suffering as savings and interest rates decline. Interest earning represented 30% of consumer income in 1989 has declined to less than 15% last year. And consumer spending won't get a boost from current home refinancing and lower fuel prices since the savings are being used to pay record consumer debt.

Consumer spending behavior will be driven by necessity rather than whim. The unlimited expectations that fueled baby boomers' spending since the 1960s has reached a plateau as they suffer a midlife economic crisis that I call yuppie shock behavior (see Chapter 6). For years, they have been trading up: new automobiles, houses, and consumer goods. Now spending patterns are going to change dramatically. Not only will they be forced to cut back, but they will be trading down. This trend will accelerate business and personal bankruptcies, which are at an all-time high. Indeed, business failures in United States is up 58.4% over 1990, and every major industrial group is involved.

GLOBAL DOWNTURN

Shoppers in other countries will spend less, adding to our troubles at home. The current economic downturn in Japan will ripple through Asia, and both British and German economic problems will spread throughout Europe. Asian dependence on U.S. markets is decreasing as intra-Asian exports, currently 40%, are expected to reach 50%. Exports to Asia had been a bright spot in our dismal trade balance. As the Far East and Europe compete with the United States for global market share with cheaper products, better technology, and more innovative products, we can expect an increase in protectionism at home and throughout the world.

In most contests, the player with "the best stuff" wins. Given the increasing fierceness of global competition, it behooves us to marshall our resources. Unfortunately, as the next chapter details, we're not in good shape. So, sadly, we're no longer a serious contender.

ENDNOTES

1.   Words and Music by Gene Raskin. TRO Copyright 1962 (renewed) and 1968 Essex Music, Inc., New York, N.Y. Used by permission.

BROKEN–DOWN ENGINES

Now we've reached the halfway house; Half the world's economy are auto related; Half the world's resources are auto devoted; and, half the world will be involved in an auto accident at some time in their lives. —Autogeddon, a fact-based poem[1]

Heathcote Williams

This chapter discusses the economic engines in manufacturing, the service sector, and high technology and explains why they can no longer provide the power to keep our plants and offices from closing. In essence, we've never recovered from the mistakes made in the 1970s.

No single fault line will devastate the economy in the 1990s more than the loss of our domestic auto industry to imported cars. The reasons for the Japanese auto success and our failure in the 1960s, 1970s, and 1980s account for why the manufacturing sector of the U.S. economy is in a tailspin.

The auto industry, the heart of our economy, has for years been developing hardening of the arteries. The massive layoffs recently announced by General Motors and others in the manufacturing sector have their roots in the 1970s, and layoffs will continue well into the 1990s.

The 1950s were the happy days for U.S. auto manufacturers and their blue-collar union employees. Then, U.S. manufacturers built three out of every four cars produced in the world, while the United States imported fewer than 1% of domestic sales. When the foreign cars appeared on the scene, Detroit could have responded by building better smaller cars, but instead U.S. automobiles grew even bigger and gaudier and sported absolutely useless tailfins. H. L. Mencken once said, "Nobody ever went broke underestimating the taste of the American public." It was this philosophy that apparently guided Detroit. But Mencken—and Detroit—were proved wrong this time.

Ironically, the Cold War played a minor role in the foreign invasion. Hundreds of thousands of U.S. troops were stationed in Europe, and they were allowed a peculiar fringe benefit. At the end of their tours of duty, they could ship home free of charge one foreign-purchased automobile. While the total number actually shipped was probably fewer than 100,000, the presence of foreign cars on U.S. highways served as rolling advertisements for Volkswagen, Austin-Healy, and other European car manufacturers, whose postwar factories were producing record numbers of vehicles. Volkswagen's advertising led the way in capturing America's imagination, and soon the VW Beetle became a kind of antisnobbery status symbol.

By the time Eisenhower left office in 1960, the United States accounted for just 50% of the world automatic market, and imports had captured a 10% share of American sales. If Detroit failed to see the handwriting on the wall, John F. Kennedy did not. Under the Kennedy administration, the military ended the free ride that GI imports had been getting to the states.

THE GREAT MISTAKES

American auto companies analyzed the threat from the small-car imports and looked at their options. They could have prevented imports from getting a foothold in the United States by producing small cars themselves. That strategy had worked quite well in the 1950s, when three compact models from Detroit knocked Japanese import sales from about 10% to 5% of the U.S. market. American auto companies could have fought the foreign invasion by using to advantage the U.S. distribution, supply, financial, and technological strengths. Foreign exporters had major disadvantages to overcome, which included such diverse areas as developing spare parts suppliers and car service networks, overcoming negative attitudes toward foreign cars among older-generation Americans, and grappling with the long distance from production to market. Moreover, some initial imports from Japan were so poorly designed that they couldn't make it up steep hills.

Alas, American companies decided against that strategy. They calculated that producing small cars would cut into the sales of big cars and would mean lower profits even if foreign competition were kept out. The rationale was that Detroit could not load a small car with high-return options such as power steering and power brakes, large V-8 engines, air conditioning, and automatic transmissions. So Detroit simply conceded the small-car market to imports. "So what?" it thought. "Let the imports hold 15% of the U.S. market because they are low-profit models." Detroit would produce a few small cars but would not spend much to develop them.

As shown in Figure 4-1, any auto analyst should have known that the future of the auto industry, from the mid-1960s on, would be in small, fuel-efficient cars. But then came the oil embargo of 1973. All across the country, millions of Americans waited in long gas lines, and the longer they waited, the more many of them calculated for the first time just how precious few miles their guzzlers could go on a tankful. Suddenly, Americans were interested in small cars in a big way!

GM, however, continued to ignore the sales charts. It did not have the product the market demanded, and sales of domestically produced cars fell sharply. Honda had the right product, and its growth was dramatic (see Figure 4-2).

By 1977 and 1978, memories of gas lines had faded, and domestic car sales rose to new heights. Detroit executives popped champagne corks and toasted their own wisdom.

Unfortunately, Detroit's success in 1977 and 1978 led it to the dangerous and erroneous industry misperception that without high energy prices, consumers felt no need to economize or buy fuel-efficient cars.

The party did not last long. A second gas crunch accompanied the Iranian revolution in the spring of 1979. But unlike the sequence of events that followed the oil embargo of 1973, this time buyers failed to return to larger vehicles after the initial shock about fuel wore off. Domestic manufacturers found themselves selling all the small cars they could produce but fewer larger models. Detroit was forced to wait for new generations of small, fuel-efficient cars that were still only on the drawing boards. In fact, Detroit had committed to spending more money on massive redesign programs than it cost to send the Apollo mission to the moon. In other words, our "can do" management was spending $1 billion for every 1/2 mile improvement in average fleet fuel economy.

FIGURE 4-1 Percent of U.S. New Car Retail Sales by Class, 1968-1976

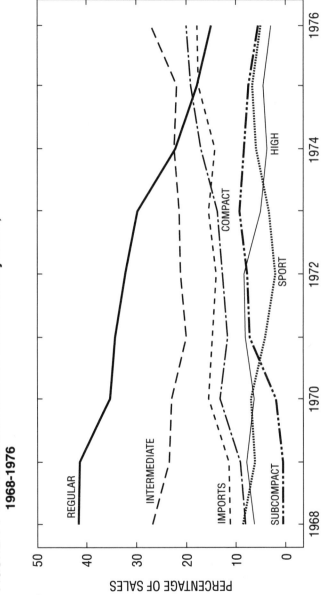

SOURCE: Motor Vehicle Manufacturers Association of the U.S., Inc.

**FIGURE 4-2 Honda and Volkswagen Sales Experience in
the United States, 1970-1983**

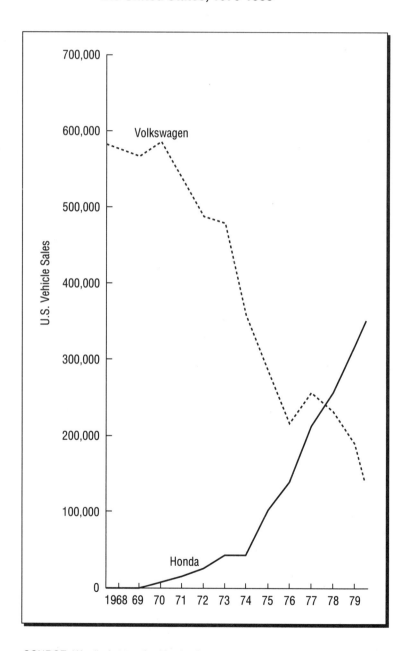

SOURCE: Ward's Automotive Yearbook

While Detroit was trying to make a U-turn, domestic car sales plummeted for four years—from 1979 through 1982. This was the longest period of falling car sales in U.S. history. Sales in 1982 were an incredible 45% below 1978 sales. Instead of meeting the challenge head on with vaunted Yankee ingenuity, Detroit instead began waving the white flag. Plant after domestic plant closed, and over 55,000 workers lost their jobs. AND as a result, the small-car fever that gripped the nation was a boon for foreign manufacturers, who had long concentrated their attention on the small-car segment of the marketplace.

Why Were the "Great Mistakes" Made?

The reason Detroit goofed was no mystery. U.S. auto management had never really understood who its customers were. It had never appreciated the fact that *drivers* are the people who count. Instead, the people Detroit sought to satisfy were the company directors, the captains of industry who met once a month to give management its report card. As market share eroded, management began increasingly to look for quick fixes to gain shareholder approval and thus hold onto their jobs for another 30 days. Accordingly, they emphasized strategies that would produce short-term profits. Rather than spending earnings on creative research and development (R&D) that could have produced new products and long-term growth, they tinkered with existing products to try to make them more attractive.

Detroit wasn't the first to substitute short-term fixes for long-term vision. Typically, U.S. businesses are managed as a series of profit centers; as a result, the preoccupation with day-to-day company finances is inordinate. When times are uncertain, the blue suits give way to the brown suits, and the accountant is king. Executives who rose from the ranks from detail-oriented disciplines—accounting, finance, law, and engineering—

tend to be "steady-state efficient," but they are hardly equipped by training or temperament to be "strategically responsive." To them, the future is next week, so they spend their days figuring out how to get the product out the door in a continuous flow. Next year, they apparently believe, will take care of itself.

But the federal government threw a monkey wrench that required the automobile industry to respond strategically. Regulation of air and noise pollution, fuel economy, and safety was universally accepted, but the piecemeal administration of these regulations by various governmental agencies produced conflicts.

Achieving one goal often interfered with meeting another. The most notable example of this conflict is that between reducing fuel emissions and improving fuel economy. Furthermore, consumer outcry over government regulation, such as the seat belt ignition interlock system, sometimes caused reversals in regulation and necessitates expensive adjustments by the industry.

If both automobile management and government agencies were shortsighted, U.S. unions proved to be no different. Unions threatened stoppages unless management granted them excessive wage and benefit packages; in fact, the unions' style seemed to demand confrontation and inflexibility. At the same time, increasingly sloppy workmanship became so well publicized that "Made in Detroit" replaced "Made in Japan" as an indicator of shoddy goods. The unions were surely aware that U.S. unit manufacturing labor costs had grown dramatically between 1975 and 1980 (see Figure 4-3). By 1980, wages of the U.S. autoworker were more than double those of autoworkers in Japan and Germany. Moreover, auto wages were 30% to 50% higher than the average U.S. industrial wage. Studies showed that the Japanese had enjoyed a cost advantage over a U.S. car of $1,000–$2,000 per vehicle. The unreasonable demands of American unions only exacerbated the diffi-

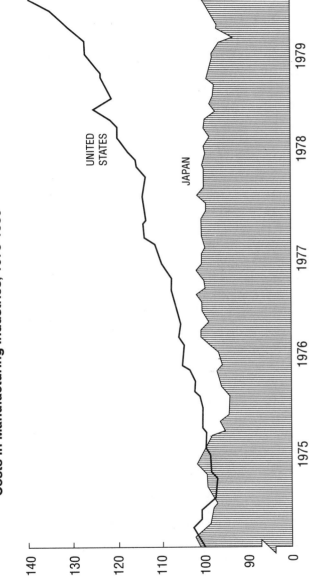

FIGURE 4-3 Comparison of Japanese and U.S. Unit Labor Costs in Manufacturing Industries, 1975-1980

SOURCE: U.S. Bureau of Labor Statistics

culty for American manufacturers of competing with foreign automakers.

The high wages paid to U.S. autoworkers helped account for the precipitous drop in U.S. productivity in the early 1970s that undercut our country's ability to compete in world markets. As we see in Figure 4-4, we were even losing the productivity race to nonindustrial Italy! And things aren't going to improve soon. The U.S. Bureau of Labor Statistics projects a continuation of declining productivity during the next decade.

However, it wasn't only that we made the wrong decisions during this critical period. Our current situation also reflects the fact that the Japanese made the right ones. They were "strategically responsive." They saw clearly the opportunities and threats of the mid-1970s and moved nimbly to maximize the former and avoid the latter.

During the 1970s, I was on several interdisciplinary teams that consulted with Japanese automakers who were considering production of their cars in the United States. The prime motive for such a dramatic change was the increasing competitiveness of their products in the energy expensive environment brought on by the oil embargo. Also, they knew that U.S. government–mandated fuel efficiency would benefit foreign companies, who were already producing small engines. U.S. automakers, they correctly surmised, couldn't do the same without expensive retooling.

In the early 1970s, foreign penetration of the U.S. market grew from less than 10% to more than 30%. The impact on the United States created political pressure to limit imports. So foreign makers took the next logical step. To protect their market share in the United States—and for both economic and political reasons—several foreign automakers thought it necessary to produce in the United States.

Consider the example of Volkswagen AG, whose popular Beetle had 5% of the U.S. market in the late

FIGURE 4-4 International Productivity Race: Increase in output per man-hour of work, 1970-1978

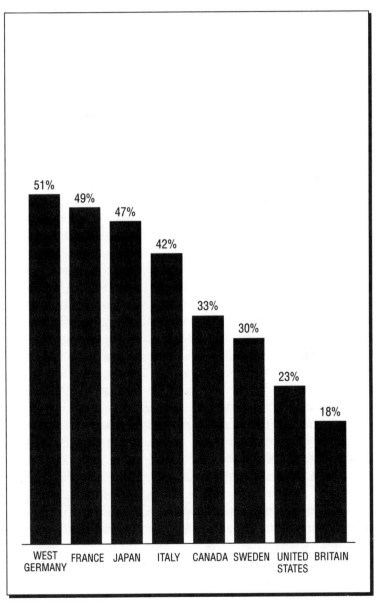

NOTE: Slower growth in productivity for United States undercuts nation's ability to compete in world markets.
SOURCE: U.S. Department of Commerce Statistics

1980s. As the car became overpriced and obsolete, VW sales dropped from close to 600,000 vehicles in 1970 to fewer than 100,000 in 1982 (shown earlier in Figure 4-2). So to regain market share and also avoid unpredictable monetary exchange problems, VW decided to build a plant in the United States. With a long history of small-car sales in the United States, the company had a chance to exploit the renewed interest in these cars. It began production in 1978. Unfortunately, it made the mistake of diluting its proven German concept of "co-determination," wherein representatives from management, unions, government, banks, and the business community serve on the supervisory board. Instead it operated like any American auto manufacturer and suddenly became involved with United Autoworkers Union (UAW) labor issues. With three quick strikes, VW management was learning the American approach to labor relations.

Honda followed VW, though its reasons were quite different. Honda's sales in the United States were increasing rapidly, from zero in 1970 to over 300,000 in 1982. Honda needed more production capacity. The company believed that the potential for exporting was severely limited and began considering a U.S. plant in 1974. At the same time, the need for energy-efficient automobiles was being sparked by the energy crisis. A four-year study by a team composed of personnel from various Honda disciplines concluded that production of their small vehicles in the United States was logical. Honda of America started production in the United States in November 1982 at its plant in Marysville, Ohio.

Start-up was slow to assure high standards of quality. The assembly plant was highly automated, featuring a Honda-designed spot welder that did 90% of the welds on the car. The plant located suppliers whom they controlled, such as Bellemar Parts and Stanley U.S.A. near the plant. It employed the efficient Japanese "just-in-time" system, where the entire length of one side of the plant is an unloading area that enables parts to be put directly into the assembly line.

It employs labor-management policies that are used in Japan. Brief team meetings are held every day to discuss production goals and suggestions for improving work on the line. Employees are rotated to different work stations every three to six months. Quality control isn't a separate, snooping department. It is the responsibility of all employees. Being well aware of the problems of dealing with UAW, Honda developed a strategy to make sure the union was kept out. Part of the strategy was a careful employment process that screened out applicants with pro-union sentiment.

By 1983, most Japanese and European firms were actively studying the feasibility of manufacturing in the United States, and today, most are producing in the United States. Their success, led by Honda, was accelerated by the great mistake of the U.S. auto executives not to enter the small-car market sooner and by the hostile labor-management relations that has led to the downward spiral of the auto industry and the scores of industries dependent on it.

THE VIRUS SPREADS

Today, other manufacturing segments such as machinery and chemicals production are shrinking due to acquisitions, restructuring, cost cutting, and the selling of unproductive assets. Experts predict that steel shipments may slump 11% and the companies could lose $1.3 billion. In the 1980s companies were able to increase productivity through capital spending and quality improvement. However, steel is getting the same price on average as it did in 1984 and thus cannot pass on its rising labor costs in the form of price increases to an ail-

ing auto industry. There has been a slowdown in imports
due to the voluntary-restraint agreements on steel imports. However, the Bush administration vows not to
renew these agreements, which could lead to foreign
dumping.

THE SERVICE SECTOR

The service sector includes transportation, utilities,
wholesale and retail trade, financial services, insurance,
real estate, and other consumer and business services.
Historically, it has provided consistent employment
growth and, unlike the manufacturing sector, has been
for the most part recessionproof. It even absorbed workers displaced from the shakeout in manufacturing and
pulled the country out of the 1981–82 recession. But the
excesses of the 1980s will continue to be paid for in the
1990s.

How Financial and Business Services Led the Economy Out of the 1981–82 Recession

Wall Street firms grew fat feasting on a takeover mania
that fed the bull market of 1983–87. Financial services
employment expanded a whopping 27%, and companies
located their expanded staffs in luxurious new offices.
They accumulated large portfolios of risky high-interest
junk bonds and bridge loans. Jobs grew at 27% in New
York. Data processing jobs grew at an annual rate of
10%, and legal services exploded to the point where the
United States now has 70% of the world's lawyers.

However, after the stock market crash in 1987, Wall
Street led a hasty, across-the-board retreat. Firms were
forced into major retrenchments, and employment
dropped 20%. As firms cut back on their deal making
and concentrate on their retail, trading, and underwrit-
ing operations, a very highly competitive environment is

emerging. American Express was hit with a 91% decline in its third quarter 1991 earnings.

Banking is in the most serious trouble, mainly because of huge loan defaults. These problems will accelerate as the economy deteriorates. An additional 340–400 bank failures are expected in the next two years. Many undercapitalized banks cannot afford the increases in Federal Deposit Insurance Corporation (FDIC) insurance, which were necessitated by billions of dollars in bad real estate loans. Even strong banks are concerned. Wells Fargo & Co, the largest commercial lender in California, has an estimated two-thirds of its commercial property loans in Southern California, which is currently feeling the impact of recession more severely than the rest of the state. The real problem for Wells Fargo is the huge amount of debt secured by improved land in projects on the market and not yet for sale. It claims only 0.13 of a percentage point in real estate lending losses over the past 16 years. Yet nonperforming real estate loans, foreclosed loans, and loans past 90 days due total $1.157 billion and suffered a 23% increase in the just one three-month period from December 1990 to March 1991.

Banks simply don't have the capital to invest and to maintain adequate reserves to cover problem real estate loans. This will remain a problem as personal savings continue to drop while cash-starved consumers empty their accounts to pay for debts. Meanwhile cautious businesses have cut borrowing for capital expenditures.

Consolidations of banks are making for fewer but bigger banks. While these mergers eventually will make the larger banks more productive as well as better able to compete against the Japanese mega banks, the announced cuts, most of which have not yet occurred, will deepen this recession. When the FDIC gave final approval to the merger of Bank of America and Security Pacific, it was in effect creating the second largest bank in the United States, with an estimated $190 billion in assets. At the same time, it was signing the pink slips for an estimated 12,000 employees which B of A said would go as part of an effort to trim $1.2 billion in annual operating costs.[2]

The Role of Residential and Commercial Construction in Providing Well-Paying, Blue-Collar Jobs During the 1980s

During the 1980s, huge commercial construction projects were built to house the growing service and high-tech sector. Developers like John Portman, Trammell Crow, and Donald Trump were helping to provide well-paying blue-collar jobs. These projects allowed younger workers opportunities to enter the building trades as new construction projects skyrocketed.

But now U.S. real estate is in the worst down cycle since the recession of 1974–76. With a 19.5% nationwide office vacancy rate, property foreclosures and developer financial problems are epidemic. Massive overbuilding and its related problems were caused by several factors, including a dramatic increase in foreign investment in U.S. real estate and significant increases in real estate lending by commercial banks and institutional pension funds.

What this means, as Adrienne Linsenmeyer observes in her article "Real Estate: The Gathering Storm,"[3] is that if the liquidity crisis facing commercial real estate today is not handled properly by the federal government, it could plunge the economy into a depression and could delay, for as much as two decades, the recovery of an industry that accounts for 25% of the domestic gross national product and two-thirds of the nation's wealth. With construction peaking in 1987, the amount of loans coming due at the banks is about to explode over the next three years. The slide of renewal rates and 15–25% vacancy rates in major cities mean there are many new buildings whose cash flow cannot cover their highly leveraged debt service. To sell those loans in today's declining market, banks would have to take write-downs of 30–50% on the asset value. Despite the magnitude of these devaluations, banks are being pressured by regulators not to refinance and prolong these bad loans, but to call them and take the write-downs. Japanese banks have also been squeezed by falling real estate values. The Bank of Japan has released $15 billion of new money to shore up the bank's dwindling reserves and avoid a U.S. style liquidity crisis. Cognetics, Inc., predicts the need for new primary office construction will be only 10% of recent years due in part to today's high vacancy and slow office growth.[4]

The Retailing Boom of the 1980s

Retail sales figures reflect a significant aspect of the health of the economy. Retailers are feeling bloated from the effects of their overexpansion in the 1980s. Sales in the 1980s grew a robust 4% annually, as the last of the baby boomers entered the work force. The 25-and-over set, which grew at 2% or more annually for most of the 1970s and 190s—boosted the retail sales of appliances, furniture, clothes, and baby gear. Unfortunately, the trends are no longer positive. The growth rate of adults 25 and over is expected to dwindle to 1% or less in the 1990s, hurting the sale of big-ticket items. Also, the growing fear of layoffs will keep consumer confidence and retail sales low.

Another legacy of the 1980s retail and construction boom is that there are too many shopping malls and shopping centers. The United States, according to the retail consulting firm Management Horizons,[5] has twice the retail space per capita as it had in 1974. That, according to Coopers & Lybrand's Bob Zimmerman, might represent an overbuilding of as much as 50%.[6] If, as predicted, the 1990s are to be the slowest-growing decade since the 1930s, the enormous shakeout in retailing will continue. Profits will diminish as retailers are forced to discount heavily while their fixed costs remain high.

Many retailers suffering under enormous debt will require refinancing to survive the tough times. Others will simply go out of business, putting tens of thousands of semiskilled workers out of work and further straining federal and state governments' meager social resources.

Why the Economy Has No Engine of Growth at this Time

Clearly, neither manufacturing nor the service sector is the locomotive that can pull us out of the recession, but what about high tech? The computer industry, the driving economic force of the 1980s, is losing rather than gaining jobs. Cuts in the thousands have been announced by giants like DEC, IBM, and Apple as well as by small parts suppliers. IBM has eliminated 53,000 jobs since 1987. Still, its profits continue to decline. From my vantage point, as a columnist who had been writing about the future for a Silicon Valley business publication for years, I've watched the problem developing. Sales have been flat at home, prices have been falling, and the makers of PC clones have made personal computers a commodity. Increased productivity of computer manufacturing has made the computer the latest high-volume electronic device to complete a premature growth phase. The rise of offshore production of computers and peripherals is likely as value-added differentiation deteriorates into a look-alike price war.

The outlook is bleak as the growing demand for high-powered, lower-margin desktop and laptop computers will continue to force suppliers and retailers to consolidate. And the European market, a major source of business for U.S. computer makers, continues weakening.

Biotech's Perceived Role as the Growth Industry for the 1990s Will Probably Never Be Realized

Biotechnology is a catch-all term used to describe a wide range of technologies that involve a wide range of industries. It includes genetic engineering to produce large quantities of valuable natural proteins and hybridoma formation for the production of monoclonal antibodies, the human body's defense against viruses and bacteria, as well as the cell fusion procedures used in plant agriculture. As a consultant to a start-up biotech company and as a contributor to a publication on the status of biotechnology, I've watched biotechnology evolve during the 1980s.

In 1987, there were over 300 companies in the field, but few, if any, were profitable. Indeed, a 1986 analysis of about 100 publicly held biotech companies by Arthur Young & Company found that of each $10 million revenues, 27% had come from contract research, 8% from interest, and only 58% from product sales industrywide. However, through venture capitalists, public stock offerings, and the like, start-up biotech companies had raised about $4 billion by early 1987.

The industry today is characterized as the last hope for investors looking for high returns as money market interest rates, real estate, and computer profits continue to drop. But the overheated market for biotech stocks and the new public offerings of a rash of start-ups have clouded the reality. The largest biotech company, Genetech, Inc., employs only 2,100 people, many of them highly skilled technicians and scientists. We will not see the explosion of biotech as a job producer. Indeed, this industry will not make a dent in the unemployment problems created by the manufacturing, service, and high-tech sectors.

Why Exports Cannot Save U.S. Industries and Produce Many New Jobs

I'm often asked if the emerging global markets are the vehicle to jump start the economy. Well, the fact is opportunities do exist overseas. In telecommunications, phone equipment exports are expected to double in the year 2000 from about $100 billion in 1991. In chemicals, 1992 is expected to produce a trade surplus of $18.5 billion compared to $19.5 billion in 91. Even machinery and steel see their fastest-growing markets outside the United States.

The problem is that for many U.S. manufacturers, making products and components abroad is almost always more profitable than making them here. Indeed, with the exception of Boeing and a few others, most manufacturing companies produce more overseas than they export from the United States. This includes Ford and many of the other heavy equipment manufacturers.

Another disturbing trend is worldwide overcapacity, as newly industrialized countries add to their manufacturing base. This includes the countries of Eastern Europe and the former Soviet Union, who will be potent competitors once they get on track. Dwindling markets and fierce global competition overseas will exacerbate the bad situation in Europe and Asia. And it's a fallacy to think the Third World and Eastern European markets will have the resources to buy American. *Our problems affect the whole world, since we are still the largest marketplace.*

A United Nation's economic study predicts worldwide slowdown and continued softness in European and Japanese economies. In Europe, an expected drop in the interest rate will increase mergers and consolidations and mean fewer jobs in the long run, increasing a growing unemployment problem. What this all means is a worldwide glut of labor and production capacity for manufactured products, causing the world to slide into a series of recessions. Only countries with broadly diversified economies that are not export dependent will make it.

Given the pressures that I have described in the preceding chapters, you may well be wondering why alarm bells are not being rung by our leaders and economic experts. Clearly, alarms should be sounding now. Why they are not is the topic of the next chapter.

ENDNOTES

1. From *Autogeddon*. Copyright © 1991 by Heathcote Williams. Reprinted by permission of Arcade Publishing.

2. This discussion draws on *The New York Times*, March 24, 1992.

3. From "Real Estate: A Global Report." *Financial World*, Vol. 160, Issue 23; Nov. 12, 1991, pp. 26-29.

4. From "Opportunities in Office and Industrial Real Estate: Finding Gold After the Rush" in *Real Estate Accounting & Taxation*. Vol. 6, Issue 3, Fall, 1991, pp. 22-31.

5. From "Retailing Challenges: Reconsidering Strategic Options" in *Executive Briefing*, Aug. 1991, pp. 7-9.

6. Ibid.

ECONOMISTS AND OTHER PUNDITS: WHY THE EXPERTS ARE MISSING IT

They were not prepared for the storm today, so they have all been thrown into great confusion. They do not possess a compass, for ordinarily when the weather is fine, they follow the old tradition and steer by the stars in the sky, without making serious mistakes regarding their direction. This is what we call "depending upon heaven for existence."

But now they have run into this bad weather so they have nothing to rely upon. It is not that they don't want to do well, only they do not know the direction and so the further they go the more mistakes they make.

Travels of Lao Can, by Liu E.
Beijing, China 1905

If, as I suggest, we are about to enter a depression of historical magnitude, why don't economists, futurists, the Federal Reserve, and politicians from both parties understand the depth of the problem? Obviously, they and I perceive the signals the economy is sending differently. In this chapter, I will discuss how the invalidated but nevertheless accepted theories of economic history have blinded today's leaders, who are still charting their course by inadequate measures and outdated techniques.

Economists love to go on programs like McNeil–Lehrer and debate ferociously over the potential effect of proposals like a cut in the capital gains tax. One says it will stimulate us right back into the happiest of economic times, while the other will smirk and suggest that his adversary has no understanding of anything even remotely economic.

The casual viewer might think these people have few beliefs and theories in common. Nothing could be further from the truth. Virtually all leading economists share one unifying belief: they make their living predicting how tomorrow will be like yesterday. Because they are forever looking backward into the mirror of the past, they do not see—indeed *cannot* see—the coming econoquake.

STRAIGHT-LINE PROJECTIONS

Economists look for past trends that can be projected to predict future economic events. This works quite well when the economy is moving relatively slowly and there are few variables, or when the variables are behaving in a reasonably predictable manner. The 1960s, for instance, made everyone look good because the trends were up, and it was quite easy to project straight-line growth. It didn't take skilled economists to produce quite accurate forecasts—most businesspeople I know were able to handle the job. At about this time economics became a growth industry. The business schools began churning out MBAs who were trained in building econometric models that base their estimates on past correlations.

RECYCLING BUSINESS CYCLES

But, as the Buddhist monks would remind us, things are always changing. So it is with our economic system. We continually follow a cycle that alternates between boom and bust, rarely achieving a balanced state where prices are stable and we are all employed. Economists believe they can predict the path of these cycles. The economic indicators which the federal government publishes monthly are supposed to forecast the cyclical ups and downs. For example, a three-month downturn in these "leading" economic indicators, such as the money supply and housing starts, indicates a recession will be upon us in six months.

WHY THESE FLUCTUATIONS

Wave-like expansion and contractions in business can be traced almost back to the founding of the United States Economists have continually seen cyclical movements in employment, factory output, interest rates, bank credit, as well as in such far-removed phenomena as marriage, birth, and divorce rates. By studying many economic time series, The National Bureau of Economic Research (NBER) believes it has identified 30 complete business cycles between 1834 and 1958 having an average length of just over four years. cycles of three to five years are called the Kitchin cycle, named for Joseph Kitchin who first wrote about them. The Kitchin cycle, which the government and the mass media most frequently cite, tracks inventories, wholesale prices, interest rates, and bank clearings.

Over the decades, Kitchin cycles have differed markedly in amplitude. Every second or third cycle has been more violent than the intervening one. Peaks which culminated in about 1899, 1907, 1913, 1920, 1929, and 1944 seem to have ended in major booms that have preceded severe declines in business. These six peaks are considered to enclose five such major cycles, lasting 45 years all together, with an average duration of 9 years. Major cycles averaging 8 to 11 years in length have been called "Juglar cycles," for a Frenchman who wrote about them over 130 years ago.

Nicolai Kondratieff, a Russian economist, found statistical evidence of cycles of even longer duration, at least in the case of commodity prices and interest rates. These cycles are purported to have an average duration of between 40 and 50 years.

Do These Cycles Really Exist?

Mainstream economists rely so much on business cycle theory for their thinking that they no longer question its existence or value as a predictor of economic events, such as the next recovery. I question its existence now very seriously, and so have others in the past.

W. Allen Wallis, former professor of statistics and economics at the University of Chicago, said flatly that they don't exist. He believes these so-called business cycles are not cycles with the rigid periodicity implied by the term "cycles," but oscillations of variable (and unpredictable) duration and amplitude. "Almost any series, if stared at long and hopefully enough begins to shape up into patterns and cycles," he states. "An enterprising new Rorschach* may some day develop a test of statistical personality based on a standard set of random serially correlated time series."

Two other respected observers believe that the business cycle which forms the basis of current economic thought and forecasting is a psychological rather than a real-world tool. They are Arthur F. Burns and Wesley C. Mitchell, former experts with the NBER, the organiza-

---

*Founder of the famous inkblot test in psychology that bears his name.

tion that studied and identified the short cycle that today's economists and politicians are patiently waiting to rebound. Burns and Mitchell warned "that when we speak of observing business cycles we use figurative language. For like other concepts, business cycles can be seen only in the mind's eye."[1]

Some cyclical theories fall of their own weight—or lack thereof. British economist William Jevons (1834–82) found a correlation between sunspot cycles of 11 years, a similar cycle of rainfall in the Ohio and Mississippi valleys, and a cycle of the same length in business conditions. A recalculation of sunspot data and the decline in the relative importance of the Ohio and Mississippi valleys as an influence on the world's wheat supply killed that theory.

Harold Barger, a former professor of money and banking at Columbia University, noted that no two cycles are exactly alike in duration, amplitude, or even in the area of the economy principally affected. Even no two Kitchin cycles, which average only four years, are exactly alike. Their peaks and valleys vary considerably, and some peaks were followed by severe financial crises while others were succeeded by declines so gradual that nobody even recognized the decline until many months later. Barger asks the obvious question: "If individual business cycles display so many differences from each other, how can we say anything useful about business cycles in general? Some writers have indeed denied the existence of cycles in business, claiming that the fluctuations we observe are essentially random in nature."[2] Barger, however, does go with the mainstream opinion. "That these wavelike movements in business are evidence of a rhythm which is worth investigation, and not simply due to chance causes."[3]

RELIANCE ON "MACRO MEASURES"

Most of what we hear in the media these days consists of economists discussing such indicators as gross national product (GNP), changes in money aggregates, and so on. Supposedly, these tell us about the health and direction of the economy. But these measures are so "macro" that observing them produces little in the way of knowledge of what's going on in the real world. The fact is that we all ought to be extremely cautious about the value of data received and used by economists, futurists, government, and other pundits.

As Burns and Mitchell noted, what we have seen over the last century and a half is not a uniform rising and falling of economic activities in unison. Instead what we have seen has been changed readings taken from many recording instruments of varying reliability. These readings have to be decomposed for our purposes; then one set of components must be put together in a new fashion. The whole procedure is far removed from what actually happens in the real world. Whether its results will be worth having cannot be assured in advance and can be determined only by pragmatic tests after the results have been attained.

This predicament is common to all observational sciences. A familiar example is meteorology. We laypeople observe the weather directly through our senses. We see blue sky, clouds, snow, and lightning; we hear thunder; we feel wind, temperature, and humidity. The meteorologist makes direct observations as well, but instead of relying upon his sense impressions, he uses a battery of recording instruments—thermographs, barographs, anemometers, wind vanes, and so on. In other words, he transforms much that he can sense, and some things that he cannot sense, into numerous sets of symbols void of all qualities of personal experience. It is from these symbols from his own station and with similar symbols sent by other observers dotted over continents that he works.

All of us can observe economic activities as easily and directly as we can observe the weather, for we have

merely to watch ourselves and our associates work and
spend. What we observe has a wealth of meanings no
symbols can convey. We know more or less intimately
the plans and problems, successes and failures of ourselves and a few associates. But we also realize what
happens to us and our narrow circle is determined
largely by what is being done by millions of unidentified
strangers. What these unknowns are doing is important
to us, but we cannot observe it directly.

Someone tending an open hearth furnace has a
close-up view of steel production. But what they see,
hear, and smell is only a tiny segment of a vast process.
They work at one furnace, but cannot see the hundreds
of other furnaces in operation in the country. And smelt-
ing is only one stage in a process that includes mining
and transporting iron, limestone, and coal; raising capital; hiring and training workers; making and selling
goods that give rise to a demand for steel; and setting
prices.

No one can personally watch all these activities. Yet
people dependent on the steel industry need an overall
view of what is happening. To get it, they, like meteorol-
ogists, use symbols that bear no semblance to actual pro-
cesses. The complex steel-making process is reduced to a
column of numbers purporting to show how many tons of
ingots have been turned out in a given area during suc-
cessive days or weeks.

We can readily see that the tonnage reports from
the complex steel operation have little connection with
the real world. Yet "the" business cycle is the cumulative
result of the combined effect of many underlying supply
and demand cycles of widely diverse businesses from
steel to beef. The price fluctuations and their effects on
the supply and demand for beef and the time it takes to
breed and bring cattle to market for all the cattle in the
country are a few factors in the cow business cycle.
Think of scores of other industries each with its own

complex cycle being combined with the cow business cycle, and you will have to agree that economists can't tell cow manure from knowledge.

University of Maryland Professor of Economics Melville Ulmer summed up my feelings about economics and the practitioners of this black art:

> Since mainstream economics is by nature dogmatic, and most often ideological to boot, experience has proved to be an ineffective teacher. Facts do not disturb deductive reason based on arbitrary assumptions. Moreover, professional reputations, including Nobel Prizes, continue to rest on faithful devotion to the sacred mysteries of mainstream methodology. The weight of such personal investments has calcified into a self-perpetuating cult, with guildlike restrictions on apprenticeships and approved research procedures. This is why no prospective turnabout appears in the offing, at least not one generated within the professional mainstream itself.
>
> The prestige of no professional group—doctors, lawyers or politicians—can plummet indefinitely without courting the complete rejection of its consuming public. Economics cannot be exempted. Competition in the world of ideas seems certain to enforce a return to standards that will insure its ultimate survival: Plain speaking, testable theories, and verifiable evidence, whether inspired by present or future dissidents from the prevailing mainstream. Until that counter-revolution arises, as it must in time, the authority of economics and economists, which has already fallen so far, will no doubt fall even lower.[4]

WHY ECONOMISTS ARE UNABLE AND UNWILLING TO FORESEE STRUCTURAL SHIFTS

During times of economic revolution, like the 1990s, it is not sufficient for our economic leaders to sit in Washington and go through the periodic ritual of observing in what direction and how far the leading economic indicators move. They are the puppeteers of the 1960s who in the 1990s still don't realize that any strings that connected their answers to our current economic problems were cut in the 1970s.

It is my thesis that in the 1970s we entered in a completely new era—an era with no historic precedent. Therefore, we must seek other ways to view our economic state.

This, of course, is what the econoquake is all about. Contemporary economists and even the doom and gloomers weren't looking in the right places in the 1970s and therefore missed the major fault lines that are affecting today's economy.

WHY STOCKBROKERS ARE MISSING THE COMING ECONOQUAKE

Brokers, like their economist kin, also look to the past to predict the future. This after-the-fact method of prediction tends to fit what has transpired into convenient correlatives and produces such diverse fancies as the "random walk theory" and stock market analysis based on the movement of the stars. At the other extreme are the analysts who often get too close to the problem and tend to forecast events based on today's news, often occasioned by a press release from one government office to another. Thus TV anchorpeople can report quite seriously, "Stocks moved lower today on news that subway workers in New York may go on strike."

We've already seen what is wrong with analyzing the past. Despite centuries of research, no one has produced a model or an approach that works! The problem with getting too close to the present is that stock market trends, moves, and activities are hyperresponsive and seldom linked to specific environments or industries. (Would people really sell Boeing because New York subway workers might strike?) Stockbrokers or economists don't have any real understanding of what truly makes companies, sectors, and industries tick. Looking at sales results and financial statements is completely frivolous. You can't develop an understanding of a living entity through analysis of a static picture any more than a doctor could diagnose a patient by looking at a picture of the patient.

WHY THE FUTURISTS HAVE MISSED IT

The big trend writers have predicted a global economic boom for the 1990s just the opposite of my predictions of economic doom for the 1990s. They sell a lot of books, but as the 1990s are unfolding the predicted boom has not yet materialized. Looking at megatrends is analogous to the economists looking at macro economic indicators. Predicting from either is not sufficient to observe the future even if it's done from the top of a high ski slope. We are in a time of economic revolution. Rather than big trends, it's the "micro trends," the small gears that we must have a grasp of to understand the direction of the economy.

They see the decline we are all feeling and experiencing as a myth. It's certainly reality to the ever-growing ranks of the unemployed, homeless, and bankrupt. They are looking in the wrong direction, at the wrong trends, and use the established economic hacks who have no handle on the economy as their expert sources. Naisbitt, for example, uses the Federal Reserve Board chairman's observation about a trend toward "downsizing of economic output;" in plain talk this simply means making things smaller and therefore easier to move around the world, a trend helpful to the global boom he predicts in the 1990s. If instead of thinking about the downsizing of packaging, Greenspan and Naisbitt were more aware about the downsizing of America's industrial base due to consolidations, acquisitions, shrinking markets, they would begin to understand how the consolidation will continue to ripple through all the business sectors causing more unemployment and business failures and inevitably leading to a long-term depression in the 1990s.

HOW I DO IT?

It is my thesis that "you have to get into it to understand it." You cannot expect to stand on Wall Street or among the eucalyptus groves at Stanford University and talk meaningfully about the U.S. economy based on what you've read, analyzed, or viewed among the trend lines or the latest M1 figures. Nor can you harken back to the nineteenth century and develop all kinds of cycle theories that supposedly shed light on past, present, and future economics. Astrology has as much meaning—probably more.

What is affecting us now and will continue to affect us throughout the 1990s is a series of trends that were taking shape in the 1970s and 1980s. These trends or fault lines will continue to delay the expected recovery until a massive restructuring of both industry and government takes place. I have followed these trends since the 1970s. My understanding of what makes the economy tick is not based on conventional approaches, yet over a decade and a half, the accurate forecasts I've made validate that I'm on the right track. I have accurately predicted the problems we are having today not because I'm smarter or because I claim supernatural gifts. It was simply a matter of my having been at the right place at the right time—in my case, working as a management consultant at SRI International, based in Menlo Park, California, and consulting to the America's midwestern industrial heartland and the Japanese. Since I contracted to be an objective outside observer with no vested interest in outcomes, I was able to trust my conclusions even though they were and still are running counter to traditional beliefs.

SRI IN THE 1970s

Stanford Research Institute in the 1970s was at the crossroads of the future. It was a place to witness the birth of new trends, technology, and disciplines years before they reached the public and the media. In the halls of this 3,000-person think tank there were many great minds—and also a few people I call "two-steppers." Two-steppers went beyond our usual activities of adding a new bell or whistle to an existing technology or writing a report on how to solve problems or identify opportunities for our diverse global client base. Two-steppers opened fresh new fields to be explored, planted, and harvested. These included people like Doug Engelbart, whose forward thinking so confounded SRI management members that they were constantly questioning the direction of his "beard and sandal" staff in what was called the Augmentation Research Center. Doug and his colleagues had spent years following a specific plan to develop automated tools to help those individuals he called "knowledge workers" and solve broad and complex global problems.

Doug Engelbart is a remarkable man. In 1969, he gave a technology demonstration in San Francisco that stunned an audience of several thousand of the best computer minds in the country. For the first time, they viewed an interactive computer with a high-resolution graphics display. At that time, computing involved using punch cards and retrieving paper printouts. Engelbart also envisioned the word processor, multiwindow screens, electronic mail, integrative system architecture, and groupware. He was, however, most revered by my children as the inventor of the computer "mouse."

Shakey the Robot was another SRI favorite of my kids in the 1970s. It was the creation of two-stepper Charlie Rosen, then fast becoming a leader in the new field called "robotics." Also at SRI was Hewitt Crane whose spectrum of talent and achievements ranged from developing the first all magnetic logic computer system to pioneering pen input computing—"electronic paper"—a two-step technology for the 1990s. And there were Arnold Mitchell in psychographics, and Joe McPherson, whose innovation search program benefited from these great minds and others.

In the area of management and economics, hundreds of professionals consulted about a broad spectrum of industry-specific concerns. The area to which I belonged, General Management Consulting Group, had a broad mandate that allowed its consultants to interact with and often lead interdisciplinary projects for large commercial and government clients worldwide. The work often involved strategic planning, another concept pioneered at SRI.

While leading a large intraindustry project for a major Midwest utility, I first became aware of some economic rumblings. The utility had invested billions for the partial construction of a nuclear power plant. Before spending additional billions, utility executives wanted an objective evaluation of how much energy their customers would require. As it turned out, while completing this study and a couple of others, I spent several years interviewing scores of senior executives representing a broad range of manufacturing and commercial businesses in America's industrial heartland.

When I wasn't working in the Midwest, I was working on large projects for Japanese auto manufacturers considering producing cars in the United States. Japanese executives from a broad spectrum of industries frequently visited SRI to keep up on the latest breakthroughs and opportunities. Typically, a senior executive would question one or more consultants, while two junior Japanese executives would feverishly write down every word consultants said.

With one project following closely upon another, there was little time to contemplate the project just completed, yet, in retrospect, I found that I was acquiring a "helicopter view" of the economic landscape. I became aware of the dissonance between the real world and the academic world of Macroeconomists. My observations in the real world and my discomfort with traditional economics encouraged me to develop an approach for forecasting and identifying the beginnings of the trends that affect our economy today. In the following section, I explain my forecasting techniques and the insights that led to its development.

LESSONS LEARNED IN THE REAL WORLD

In the past, utility companies predicted growth in energy demand by developing formulas that connected energy growth to macroeconomic parameters such as GNP, population, and employment. Projections about energy needs of a particular industry were viewed as a multiple of GNP growth. For example, food industry growth might be 0.4 times the growth rate of GNP and chemicals 1.5 times the growth rate.

From my fieldwork, however, I observed that such historically macroeconomic-based industry predictions were no longer accurate in the 1970s though they may have worked in the 1960s. I had learned firsthand that companies are as individual as people are. The factors affecting the success or failure of companies, even within the same industry, can be quite different. I also observed that most of the determinants were not the type of data collected or analyzed by economists and others charged with determining our economic direction. Table 5-1 lists some of the factors that determine economic success at the company level.

Quite independent of company or industry, the bottom line was that the companies interviewed had no need for additional energy capacity since most were forecasting minimal or no long-term growth for their smokestack industries. That may not sound like a major observation in today's economic news. I concluded that the manufacturing sector of the U.S. economy had peaked and was not likely to rise again in the foreseeable future. This was not popular with a client with a $4 billion bet who was hoping that I was wrong. Unfortu-

TABLE 5-1 Factors That Determine Economic Success at the Company Level

KEY INDICATOR LEGEND	KEY INDICATOR LEGEND
01 New Products/Services	21 Time Utilization
02 New Markets	22 Union Problems
03 % Distribution Controlled	23 Turnover
04 Market Share	24 R & D Productivity
05 Market Maturity	25 Environmental Factors
06 Sales Volume	26 Maintenance
07 Competition	27 Distribution/Handling Costs
08 Customer Demographics	28 Government Protection
09 Customer Psychographics	29 Social Pressure
10 Perceived Value of Product or Service	30 Liability Problems
	31 Political Clout
11 Service or Product Necessity	32 Government Stability
12 Availability of Used Equipment	33 Political Unrest
13 Sense of Urgency	
14 Strategic Responsiveness	
15 Structural Responsiveness	
16 Flexibility	
17 Experience	
18 Cost of Operations	
19 Control of Production	
20 Quality Concerns	

SOURCE: Minkin Affiliates

nately for the utility, I was right, and their macroeconomic projections proved a very costly mistake.

Of course, it is very unusual and may even seem un-American for executives who know their companies are in deep trouble to share their worries with shareholders whose bucks are keeping many sinking ships afloat.

The real world was telling me that things had turned bad. It would be years before the macro indicators sensed trouble.

MY FORECASTING TECHNIQUE

Based on what I learned from the field, I developed a simple and logical approach to forecasting. I call this six-step model the Econo 2000 system and have been using it successfully for over a decade.

Step 1. Identify the two or three company-specific factors that determine how a company will fare.

Step 2. Determine how those factors will be affected by a future scenario that predicts declining growth.

Step 3. Make predictions based on the interaction between the determinants and the scenario.

Step 4. Analyze the ripple effects of the declining growth scenario on other companies, industries, and business sectors.

Step 5. Roll up your sleeves and estimate the impact on sales for all companies in your sample.

Step 6. Compile these company-specific forecasts, and you arrive at a very accurate industry forecast.

Table 5-2, which predicts 1985 sales trends for three automobile manufacturers, illustrates the first four steps of this technique.

TABLE 5-2 ECO 2000 Simplified Example

COMPANY/ DIVISION	PREDICTION	KEY INDICATORS	EFFECT OF ECO 2000 ASSUMPTION	RIPPLE EFFECT
BMW	Increased sales through 1985; larger share of declining market from 1986.	Perception of quality, status	Fewer car sales; more business failures; fewer high-end purchases	Negative for machinery segments, fabricated metals, primary metals.
Cadillac	Steady decline from 1983.	Perception of quality, status	Fewer car sales; more business failures; fewer high-end purchases	Negative for regional service sectors.
Volkswagen	Decline from 1983.	Perception of quality, labor relations.	Fewer car sales; more business failures; fewer high-end purchases	European and U.S. auto, machinery, fabricated metals and primary metals suffer.

SOURCE: Minkin Affiliates

Step 1

The key indicators for BMW (see Table 5-1, column 3) are perception of status, perception of quality, and demographics. For Cadillac, the indicators of success or failure are the same. The key difference is that the demographics and perceptions of quality and status were positive for BMW and negative for Cadillac. In the 1980s, the [25–44] age group was the largest growing and also the one that bought the most cars. The BMW was becoming the status symbol for these yuppies, while Cadillac was considered an old person's car. German car quality was perceived as excellent, while there were doubts about the inferior fit and finish of U.S. cars. *It is important to note that these major factors for success or failure were not and are still rarely tracked by economists.* The key VW indicators were perceptions of quality and labor relations. The aging Beetle needed to be replaced by a new family of vehicles. VW's decision to open a plant in the United States using the United Autoworkers (UAW) gave rise to public concern that VW quality would suffer. Among the indicators of VW success or failure were the difficulties VW experienced in its dealings with the UAW. VW used UAW workers to build a mini-pickup and the Rabbit.

Step 2

Column 4 shows the effect of the Econo-2000 scenario that envisions a shrinking industrial base, more unemployment, and less discretionary income. The effect on all carmakers is a decline in total car sales, production of smaller and less expensive cars, more competition, and failing or merging automakers.

Step 3

Therefore, I predicted (see Column 2) that BMW would get a larger share of the declining high-end market, that

Cadillac sales would continue to decline as its regular customers die off without replacements, and that VW sales would continue to decline, with increased domestic and offshore competition.

Step 5

Column 5 shows the ripple effect of these predictions on other sectors of the economy. My bottom-up predictions were, of course, more accurate than my colleagues, which still relied on straight-line growth projections in a world that is changing irreversibly. Explaining these changes and recommending specific positive actions we can take not only to survive the econoquake but take advantage of the opportunities it presents forms the remainder of this book.

ENDNOTES

1. From *Statistics: A New Approach* by W. Allen Wallis and Harry V. Roberts. The Free Press of Glencoe, Inc., Brooklyn, New York, 1963, p 562.

2. From *Money, Banking, and Public Policy* by Howard Barger. Rand McNally Company, Chicago, 1962, p. 422.

3. Barger, Ibid.

4. From "Economics in Decline" in *Commentary*, November, 1984, New York, N.Y. pp. 42-46.

PART II

IMPLICATIONS, RECOMMENDATIONS, AND OPPORTUNITIES

HOW THE ECONOQUAKE WILL CHANGE SOCIETY

*That the birds of worry and care fly above your
head, this you cannot change. But that they build
nests in your hair, this you can prevent.*

Chinese proverb

*You cannot treat destiny. [The best you can do in
bad times is] to keep abreast of the incurable.*

E. M. Cioran

Throughout history, powerful forces have changed the
future directions of civilizations, affecting the quality of
life for all generations to come. Some of the forces behind
these changes were quite apparent to those who lived
through them: wars, famines, plagues, and major scientific, engineering, or technological breakthroughs.

At other times, however, we failed to realize the
changes a force was making in our society even as those
changes were occurring. The automobile, for example,
made possible the suburban shopping center. But as it

did so, it caused the erosion of core city shopping districts and contributed to urban blight. It enabled us to live farther from our work, but only too late did we realize that one of the prices we would have to pay would be clogged freeways and poisonous, brown sky.

Even subtler, less apparent forces had significant impacts though they were unrecognized at the time. Their effects were recognized only after the fact by a later generation, even though they were often greater—either more beneficial or more devastating—than the effects occasioned by traumatic events. The Dark Ages, the Renaissance, and the early history of Christianity had undeniable impacts on the future of the world and everyone in it, but in the early stages, those who would be most affected were completely unaware that their future and that of their children were to be dramatically altered.

We live in such a period today. Seemingly unrelated events now taking place are actually interrelated and will have an impact on the world that will last for generations. In this chapter we will paint a picture of the 1990s by looking at the multiple forces that are already shaping our future.

THE FORCES SHAPING OUR FUTURE

The Global Economic Depression

As the shockwave from the econoquake continues to batter the nation, the United States finds itself confronted on every front by forces it no longer controls. The traditional economic policies fail and wreak havoc on the public. We have a growing sense of hopelessness as we listen to continuing negative news about layoffs and plant closings. Economic depression and decay begin to affect our daily lives as we struggle to cope. How did the world leaders fail us? We feel victimized and angry. The global economic boom Naisbitt and the Kiplingers predicted for the 1990s is quickly turning out to be a pipe dream as we awake to the reality of the econoquake.

The Baby Bust Generation

The American dream has turned into a nightmare for people under 30. These 75 million Americans will be the first to lose the race for prosperity. They will be the first U.S. generation not to match their parents' standard of living. As discussed in Chapter 5, the economic engines necessary to pull us out of the recession are broken. In the 1970s, manufacturing, the wonderful high-wage machine, started to sputter, and in the 1980s, foreign competition permanently eliminated millions of jobs. This critical damage to America's industrial heart lay undetected as the service sector became the engine of growth and created most of the new jobs. But in the 1990s, employers struggling to survive have had to hold the line on payroll costs. Older workers whose incomes and savings had grown during the past two decades have been temporarily insulated from economic suffering.

Young families, however, are in economic free-fall. True, not everyone is suffering. A large percentage of professionals, engineers, programmers, technicians, and some financial types are doing well. But for millions, both the present and the foreseeable future are bleak. The median inflation-adjusted income of families headed by someone under 30 is now 13% lower than families earned in 1973. As expected, the 14% of families headed by college graduates are better off. But for the less educated majority, times are much worse. Real income for under-30 families headed by high school graduates has fallen 16%. And the incomes of high school dropouts and blacks have dropped a staggering one-third, at a time when the cost of housing has shot out of sight.

Like the youngest members of the baby-boom generation before them, the busters will put fewer dollars into the economy. During the ten-year period beginning in 1980, home ownership among the younger baby boomers fell by more than seven percentage points to 54%. As the busters enter the 1990s with reduced incomes, they will continue to buy fewer high-ticket items needed to spark economic growth. And plans about college for their kids and savings for their retirement have become little more than impossible fantasies.

The busters' most obvious problem is that only low-paying jobs are available. When the manufacturing sector began to shrink, the proportion of 30- to 62-year-olds in the work force fell from 30% to 25%. Since the unions insist on seniority, the last hired is usually the first fired, and the share of employed men under 30 dropped twice as fast, from 28% to 19%. The survivors who still have a job and those lucky enough to find jobs are getting less pay.

The unions, to secure their jobs and retirement, made concessions that allowed for so-called two-tier wage scales which pay new and usually younger workers at a lower rate for the same job. To compensate, the busters have turned to the service sector in search of a paycheck. But these jobs pay 15% to 33% less than the factories. One factor for the lower wage scale is the growing use of part-time and temporary jobs, which pay 40% less per hour on average than full-time work. Eighty out of every 100 people who earn the $4.25 minimum wage have "jobs" in the service sector.

Implications. So young Americans are in serious trouble, and unfortunately things are going to get much worse as job layoffs ripple through the economy. The children of the busters will increasingly live in poor households—nearly one in five children already does. These children will become an increasing burden on our health care and education systems. They are more likely to require special education programs that are mandated by many states. In New York State it costs as much annually to provide special education services to a student as to send a student to Harvard.

Women will be particularly hard hit. Single mothers head 24% of these young families, and working women earn only 65% of what men do. Pressure on marriage due to severe economic problems is causing an increase among the number of women and children being abused. There will be fewer and later marriages as financially secure mates become more difficult to find. The homeless populations will continue to swell. There are an estimated 90,000 homeless in New York, although the city officially acknowledges only 25,000. I predict these numbers will triple in the next couple of years. We are beginning to see sights not seen since the Great Depression in most of our cities: scores of people begging for handouts, others wearing signs that they are willing to work for food.

Minorities

The melting pot has boiled over. A massive demographic force in the econoquake is the rapid growth of racial minorities. Already 25% of Americans identify themselves as Hispanic or nonwhite. By 2000, if current trends persist, nearly one in three Americans will be a minority. The Hispanic population will further increase by about 21%, the Asian by 22%, and blacks by about 12%. By 2030, due to their higher birth rates, one-third of the population will be Hispanic, black, and Asian. While California is leading this trend, by the end of the decade, 92% of us will be living in counties made up of at least 30% minorities and will eventually have a majority of minorities. In California, white students are already a minority. By 2056, white residents will be the minority in the United States.

The econoquake will hit some minorities very hard, particularly the under-30 black and Hispanic group. These groups are more likely to be deficient in job skills. Indeed, the Hispanic 50% school dropout rate is the highest in the country. With more competition for even unskilled jobs from better educated whites and Asians, they will have to rely on their growing presence in U.S. politics to achieve their demands for job preference and continued government services. The outlook for blacks is particularly bad. In part, this reflects the higher share of young black families headed by young single mothers—58% versus 16% for whites. There are also twice as many black teenage pregnancies as whites. A majority of welfare recipients receiving general assistance (GA) are black men in urban areas with staggering unemployment rates. The depression will reinforce these negative trends. Asian Americans represent a large proportion of college graduates particularly in science and engineering disciplines and thus will continue to fare better than other minorities during the tough times ahead.

Implications. The depression will provide the heat that will cause the melting pot to boil. As the economic problems intensify, whites will rebel against the minority preferences in college admissions, government contracting, and hiring. They will complain that the pendulum of racial prejudice has swung so far that it is now discriminating against whites. Tensions between whites and minorities will increase when politicians and angry taxpayers try to cut affirmative action and social service programs that they perceive are aimed at minorities. Unfortunately, it may be a no-win situation vis-à-vis economic savings, since cuts in social services would just move the problem to the streets, where it would cause increased crime and emergency room admissions.

Nor will the tensions be only between minorities and whites. With the fast-growing Hispanic and Asian populations and the broadening of affirmative action programs that benefit white women, minorities will fight among themselves for a larger share of shrinking resources.

There will be continued efforts to make Spanish our second language. This emphasis on multicultural differences will continue, and a more accurate symbol of U.S. society will be a patchwork quilt where people retain their language, culture, and customs and remain perpetual outsiders rather than as the melting pot when earlier waves of immigrants melded together. Sustaining a truly multicultural society historically has proved very difficult. The breakup of the Soviet Union into homogeneous ethnic conclaves is the most recent example of trend toward ethnic isolation.

The "Browning of America" will alter everything in society—politics, education, the world of work, and our values and culture. Expect the econoquake to pull apart the seams of this patchwork quilt as the gap between the rich and poor widens. I predict growth in the underground economy. Expect more consumers to make their purchase at large flea markets, out of car trunks, through garage sales, and off stands rather than at retail stores with high overhead and taxes. Both the Hispanics and Asians are familiar with these markets, which are popular gathering places to meet, shop, and eat. Cash is king, and growing numbers of people will work "off-the-books," thus undermining the foundations of federal, state, and local taxing schemes.

Immigrants

The United States, which is a nation of immigrants and descendants of immigrants, will continue to be deluged by economic refugees from all over the world who will further compete with those already here for a decreasing number of jobs, thus further straining limited social resources. A new immigration law enacted in the fall of 1990 raised the number of immigrants that will be allowed into the United States each year. Expect immigration lawyers to do well as the number of illegal immigrants entering the United States will continue to increase.

More Stratification According to Race

As the earning power of minorities decreases during the econoquake, society will become even more stratified according to race. In 1967, the top 20% of the population had 40% of the income and the bottom 20% had 6%. By 1987, the gap had widened with the percentages changing to 43% and 4.6%, respectively.

Political Clout. Asians, African Americans, and Hispanics will seek greater political influence commensurate with their growing share of the U.S. population.

Women Between 1990 and 2005

The Bureau of Labor Statistics projects a 26% increase in the women's labor force. However, this rate of growth is slower than that in the 1975–1990 period. Also, women will be more represented in top-level corporate positions. The bad news is there may be an increase in abuse of women and children as continued economic problems increase psychological stress.

Decline of the Cities

As corporations continue to decline and others move to the suburbs, many of the largest cities will face continuing loss of jobs, taxes, and upscale urbanites. As the suburbs expand, they will continue to provide more jobs than our cities. We will see our once-great cities as abandoned, burned-out shells where the homeless will congregate.

The End to Baby Boom Optimism

The 76 million in the baby-boom generation are about to have a midlife crisis. The post–World War II baby boom has had and will continue to have a profound impact on American society and the economy. This will continue to be true as the oldest baby boomers turn 46 in

1992. While the rest of the population is predicted to grow between 4% and 7% over the next ten years, the ranks of the baby boomers, especially those between 35 and 54, will increase by 28%. This group in the year 2000 will account for two thirds of the U.S. population and will control more than half the nation's spending power.

In the late 1980s, baby boomers bought the American dream scenario, and like the Japanese, their confidence in the future was high. But it was way out of line with the economy, which was already on the way down. True, over the past 15 years, the number of households with annual incomes in excess of $50,000 has nearly doubled, and it is predicted to almost double again by the year 2000. In most cases, a wife's second paycheck moved the family into the $50,000-and-over category. With more income, these affluent, maturing householders were buying homes, cars, and other consumption items as if economic growth would last forever. The pundits therefore were predicting the 1990s would become the peak years for consumer spending.

Unfortunately, the boomers, now 28 to 46 years old, are beginning to encounter the econoquake in the 1990s, while at the peak of both their affluence and their family responsibilities. Many are totally unprepared for tough times ahead. For almost 15 years since the Vietnam war, the boomers have had little confidence in the country's institutions—government, big business, and even universities. Now their lack of confidence has finally spread to their own financial well-being and hopes for the future. Their confidence as consumers is very low, and it's not going to rise much, even if the economy stages a brief recovery. What we are seeing is a permanent decline in consumer expectations.

Yuppie Shock

When this brief recovery is over, and the econoquake hits in earnest, white-collar baby boomers are going to be just as permanently scarred as their parents were by the Great Depression. This is going to turn into the "just getting by" generation. With the economy collapsing around them, they will have no expectations of income growth. Instead, people will try to hold onto what they have. That means people are going to spend less and save more, and the saving is going to be real saving, not just put into a bigger house. Most people will start focusing on basics and safety rather than risk. Like past generations coming out of the depression, Americans whose lives are wrecked by the econoquake will focus on trying to make their children's lives better rather than expecting to lead good lives themselves.

Opportunities and Implications. Cultural values will shift. The concept of satisfaction will become more important than satiation. People will aim for control of one's own jobs rather than trying to make it to the top on somebody else's terms. As the largest group in the U.S. population, boomers will compete for a dwindling number of job promotions in a declining economy. The boomers are a generation of large numbers and some shared experience, and therefore were considered a marketer's dream. However, the reality is that they represent a range of differing outlooks and life-styles. There are new agers, yuppies, single-parent households, Vietnam vets, and draft dodgers in the baby-boom generation. Marketing will change as advertisers shift their appeal to values rather than competitiveness or maximizing pleasure. The need is to stress quality and value rather than indulgence and luxury. Companies which keep trying to build their message on snob appeal, without offering true value, are going to find themselves in real trouble.

In times of hardship and downward mobility, marketers will have to focus on things that make people feel better. In the depression it was the movies that provided people with escapism. Now it may be travel or computer games.

In middle age, durability, comfort, and practicality are important. Levi Strauss & Company recognized these preferences and successfully introduced a line of easy-care action slacks that are conservative, comfortable, and cut for a mature man's body. Food companies are emphasizing products low in fat, sugar, salt, and cholesterol. Boomers are well educated; consequently they spend freely on educational toys and tutoring services for their children. Sharper Image Corp. and other companies are appealing to the boomers' ecological concerns. Financially, there will be a shift from carefree spending to investing in stocks and money market mutual funds and reducing credit card debts. Real estate investment will be reduced as ways to build wealth in favor of more liquid investments (see Chapter 8). The baby boomers will be looking for opportunities and financial products that will help them achieve security for themselves and their families.

Aging Boomers

Only half of the boomers will find retirement affordable at age 65 according to a survey of actuaries. *Warning:* There will not be enough workers to support the social security benefits because of the enormous number of baby boomers who will reach age 65 between 2010 and 2018. Baby boomers need to start saving now for their retirement, thus opening up markets for retirement planning services and long-term disability insurance. Health and nutrition will provide major opportunities, including products and services that will help people look and feel young, and convenience will drive many purchasing decisions. Over 1 million Americans spent an estimated $1.75 billion on cosmetic surgery in 1988. A study found that 45% of plastic surgery patients earn less than $25,000 and 53% are under age 39. Consumer demand for bifocal eyeglasses will grow rapidly. Health insurance agencies selling policies for individuals will do well. Many baby boomers tended to delay childbearing until their thirties and will have dependent children in their households later in life than did previous generations. There will be opportunities for child care services as both parents continue to work. The baby boomers are a generation absorbed in family life. For many couples, a two-income marriage is essential to buying a house and raising a family. New households will be formed at a much slower pace in 1990 than in the previous two decades when baby boomers were establishing homes. Around the year 2010, family life will recede, and living alone will dominate the nation.

Politics

The econoquake will turn baby boomers from progressives to neoconservatives. Only as the economy continues to stagnate and conservative measures for recovery prove futile, pushing the boomers more firmly into the working class will the political pendulum swing more to the progressive side. Boomers will try to cash out from large metropolitan areas and move to rural states. There they can reduce their overhead and avoid growing urban tax bills. With luck, they will sit out the econoquake while they commune with nature and their children telecommunicate via laptop computers and modems. The continued loss of the middle class from the cities will hasten urban decline. New York has lost 100,000 jobs since 1987, and like many U.S. cities will continue to cut services. *How many more empty commercial buildings must there be before people believe the econoquake has started?*

The Aging Face of America

One of the most important trends that will collide with the econoquake will be the aging of the U.S. population.

Indeed, over the next half century, the populations of many developed countries will decline in size and become predominantly aged. In the United States people are living longer, and both the 55–74 and the 75–84 age groups will include larger and wealthier segments of the U.S. population by the year 2000. By about the year 2030, 21% of the U.S. population will be over 65, and there will be more people 65 years of age and older than there will be under 18. Today, as a result of pension benefits and increasing social security payments, the aging U.S. consumer is apt to be less poor than the average U.S. citizen. If per capita income is considered instead of household income, on an after-tax basis, the 55–64-year-old group has the highest per capita income of any age group. However, an aging America will impose substantial economic costs, many of which will be born by employers who will be increasingly hard pressed as health care premiums continue to rise along with the expense of funding their pension systems. All this added overhead with decreasing cash flow due to the early effects of the econoquake will force employers to shift more medical costs to employees and to cut back on retiree health benefits.

Older people, like younger people, are diverse in terms of health, living arrangements, income, and personal and social resources. Although 80–85% of persons 65 years of age and over have one and sometimes more than one chronic illness, the majority of elderly are healthy enough to lead independent lives with a minimum of assistance. At the present time, about 60% of the U.S. elderly are the "young-old," those between ages 65 and 74. Most of this group is without any functional limitations.

The family currently is the primary caregiver for the elderly, assisted to some extent by neighbors and friends. The growing number of working women, the changing family structure, and the depression will make it very difficult to continue to provide this aid without more assistance from government and community support groups. Indeed, a growing trend is what hospital staffers call "granny dumping"—abandoning elderly people in hospital emergency rooms under the pretext of illness, usually by relatives who are too poor, tired, or stressed to continue providing care. With most middle-aged women in the paid work force, we can expect "elder care" to be one of the benefit options requested along with child care.

What's a working couple to do with a child and a granny between 9 and 5? A growing trend is aimed at stimulating contact between the young and the old. One such effort is a day care center set up by Stride Rite Corporation that combines two centers, allowing easy mingling between 55 children and 24 elders over 60. Psychologists point out that old people and youngsters have much to offer each other.

Opportunities and Implications. Health care systems will be strained because the elderly are the biggest users of health care. The sheer numbers of elderly projected suggest a greatly expanded need for social services. The demand for nursing homes and hospices will dramatically increase.

Life care communities and shared housing where residents have their own houses or apartments, plus nearby access to medical treatment, meals, and recreation, will be popular options. And hospitals and nursing homes looking for new profit centers will provide day care services for the elderly. We can expect life expectancy to increase due to breakthroughs in biotechnology, disease prevention, new computer and mechanical devices and instruments, and new kinds of drugs.

Changes in age and population will require new products and services. Retail stores should be aware of the needs of older customers and remember that service, accessibility, comfort, and security are key concerns of older shoppers. Clean, easily accessible bathrooms, increased lighting, easy-to-read size and price stickers, and color-coded signage are appreciated by senior shoppers. These customers value quality, customization, fast response and delivery, and personalized service.

A number of media that traditionally targeted mass markets will refocus their content to appeal to an older, more financially secure audience and there will be a growth of new media directed at these markets.

Retirees will compete with younger age groups for jobs and government spending. People over 65 receive 29% of federal spending while children under 18 get 7%. The main reason for the high senior spending is the indexing of social security benefits to the cost of living. Proposals to raise the tax on social security benefits that exceed an individual's lifetime contribution are being studied. But politicians know that seniors more consistently exercise their right to vote and are very careful about what they say that would displease seniors.

It is estimated that over 1 million Americans over 50 want to return to work. This group, which boasts substantial skills and education, is also very flexible about conditions of employment. More than half already have health insurance and wouldn't require additional coverage. This group will continue to grow and compete with younger workers, minorities, and immigrants for fewer and fewer jobs. The antiaging market will grow. Sales of Retin A, an antiwrinkle product, increased from $33.5 million in 1987 to $115 million in 1988. Many older consumers do not want to deny their age. Rather they want products and services that enhance and refine what they have.

Age Discrimination

Tough economic times will require continued work force reductions, and often the most tempting targets are older, highly paid workers. These workers, like minority groups, are increasingly going to the courts when they feel discriminated against. The Equal Employment Opportunity Commission (EEOC) expects to receive nearly 17,000 age discrimination suits in 1991. The trend will likely continue. The American Association of Retired People says that requests for information on fighting job bias have jumped 55% in the last two years.

Dying

Two related trends require a look at dying. First, the increase in longevity means that people are older when they die than they were in earlier times when most deaths occurred in infancy and young adulthood. Second, today more people typically die from distressingly prolonged chronic diseases rather than die quickly from pneumonia and other acute infections. The cost of health care for the terminally ill has raised questions that will continue to be debated in the 1990s. When, if ever, should life support systems be withdrawn? Does a "living will" have any force in law? Will health insurance cover the costs of hospice care?

As we have seen, no one will be immune from the effects of the econoquake. It will affect various segments of society differently, but from birth to death, all of us will feel it.

BUSINESS IMPLICATIONS AND GROWTH OPPORTUNITIES

But we've always done it that way.

**Epitaph of many companies
in the 1990s**

The wolf eats because it has legs.

Old Russian proverb

Doing well in business in the 1980s was easy. It seems customers were buying almost any product or service at inflated prices. Department managers were adding to staff in anticipation of continued growth. But today those recently hired staff members and their bosses are spending their lunch hours and an ever-greater part of their business day networking with friends and associates to find more secure positions as the business locomotive runs out of steam.

The dynamics of doing business will continue to change as each of our industry sectors peaks in sales and shipments. Besides the right products, the businesses that make it in the 1990s will require special managers using new management tools and techniques to succeed—or even just survive—through difficult times. In this chapter we'll look at the business management styles that contributed to the mess we've gotten into. Then we are going to present a management consulting tool kit that will enable you to overcome these problems and prepare yourself and your company for the 1990s.

RECENT BUSINESS MANAGEMENT STYLES

Companies that are strategically and structurally unresponsive will become extinct in the 1990s. I have asked and been asked many times, "Why can't business executives feel and react to the econoquake's shock wave?" Good question. They aren't stupid people, and yet top management and their advisors—their consultants and economists and corporate planners—continuously miss the warning shock wave rumbling all about them. I answer the question with a theory I've developed, which I call the AFE theory. AFE stands for "arthritic freaking elephant." That's a term I heard one corporate president use to describe his own multibillion-dollar company.

AFEs suffer from a serious malady: "strategic unresponsiveness," which is a polite way of saying the management simply cannot see what's going on outside its own boardroom. They don't have the sharp corporate eyes needed to identify how changes in demographics, life-styles, technology, and politics are affecting their companies. The most dramatic example of this is the American automobile industry in the mid-1970s, which we've referred to elsewhere in this book. It didn't need 20-20 corporate vision to know that gas guzzlers were dinosaurs. The assembly worker on the line, the housewife in Topeka, the migrant farmer in California—they all knew this. But somehow the Roger Smiths of America either couldn't or wouldn't face the inevitable. The legacy of that at GM this year is a loss not in the millions, but in the *billions.*

Large companies in mature industries tend to be steady-state efficient. By this I mean they have become very good at getting parts, cars, or trucks out the door. But as they matured from their early entrepreneurial years—if they ever were entrepreneurial—their managers lost the ability to sense market changes and to react to the needs of the marketplace. Most U.S. companies are managed by caretakers, not risk takers. The risk takers that built the companies died off a long time ago. They've been replaced by so-called "professional managers," people who do not know, and probably never will know, the business as an entrepreneur. Most of these managers are MBAs from our top schools, all shaped by the same cookie cutter.

They are the numbers-oriented "quants" who see business as a series of quantitative decision sets. They spend their executive time pouring over spreadsheets that represent some corporate planner's misguided view of reality, but in fact bear little resemblance to the real world. They take a management-by-objectives (MBO) short-term view of the world, which says that planning is strictly a top-down process, devoid of any feedback from the people who know best, the troops on the line and the consumers in the market.

While at SRI, a visiting strategic planning executive from a large European food company shared a story of how not having sharp eyes proved embarrassing and costly to a U.S. corporate giant that lost out to a Japanese trading company bidding on one of the first major telecommunications projects in Europe. The Japanese company won the bid because its executives started thinking about telecommunications, then a new field, *12 years before the bidding process began.* Seven years before the bidding, this Japanese trading company had gathered all the information it needed about this new field by tapping the expertise of consultants, visiting telecom equipment suppliers and trade shows, and pur-

chasing all the major studies in the field. Five years before the bid it learned that there was going to be a need
for such a system in Europe. Four years before, it focused on the postal service in Belgium as the group that
would install the system, so its managers visited Belgium. Three years before, it brought the Belgian "team
members" to Japan and jointly started designing the
system for them. Two years before the bidding, the U.S.
quants finally learned there was going to be a project
and requested the specifications, which were designed
around the system jointly developed with the Japanese.

In this example of strategic unresponsiveness, the
competing American firm, like so many others, could not
liberate itself from an all-consuming concern with short-
term rewards and the MBO approach that the Japanese
Company credited as the reason for its success.

The executives of the Big Three auto companies have
raised AFE management to an art form. In the face of
quite contradictory evidence, all three continued to build
cars that were clearly out of step with the desires of marketplace. The signals were clear. Reality only dawned, and
was accepted with excruciating reluctance, after the entire
industry took a clobbering. It was very sobering to hear in
the 1980s a top executive of one of the Big Three berate
the American public for their condition. The American consumer, said he, "let us down" by not buying Detroit's cars.
This executive, a charter member of the AFE Hall of
Fame, was convinced that the disloyal U.S. consumer owed
him and his company something.

PROBLEM: PRUNING DEADWOD AT THE TOP

Often the company management may clearly see the
threats and opportunities facing their organization. However, an entrenched, shortsighted CEO or board chairman
stands in the way of change. A manager I met from a
major U.S. tire company told me that although the company

had a good year, he knew its market had matured and that growth couldn't continue. Ironically, the problem was the industry's quality was just too good. Today's radial and ordinary passenger car tires last thousands of miles longer than their tube-filled ancestors, so a passenger car could go its entire life on as few as two sets of tires.

When I asked him what he was doing about it, he told me, "Nothing." And nothing would be done, he said, until the company president retired in three years. This CEO may have known that he should have been thinking about investing in a new business, or a new plant, or a new technology, but he also knew that the board was evaluating him not on how he was preparing the company to cope with the next decade, but on how healthy last quarter's P&L looked. Driven by the same survivor instinct that guides altogether too many CEOs, he spent his days figuring how to make the company appear profitable for his remaining term. As for the future, well, that would be somebody else's problem.

A good product and top-dollar advertising have also covered up a lot of bad management in the past. As a management consultant, I am constantly amazed by how poorly run some of the companies with the best public images really are. Some products have done extraordinarily well in the past not because of good management, but in spite of incredibly bad management. As a result, these leaders become jaded and believe continued success is inevitable due to their astute stewardship. Like royalty these CEOs, owners, and board chairmen make most of the corporate decisions themselves while treating company executives as robots, whose only function was to do exactly what they were told and no more. They deal directly with everyone in the organization, rarely delegating authority. They feel invincible since their product has been selling well, and they take most of the credit for the success.

Early in my career, I worked with Coca-Cola Bottling Company of New York, at that time the world's largest bottling company. As a young MBA student, I was intrigued with the day-to-day dynamics between a crusty old board chairman whose family owned lots of Coca-Cola stock and a management team led by a forward-thinking CEO. Having been recently hired, I was introduced to the chairman by a very senior executive who then proceeded to tell me how the chairman, while an executive at the Coca Cola Company in Atlanta in the early 1930s, made a key decision that helped launch Pepsi-Cola. The story, which I cannot verify independently, is that some of the marketing staff at Coke came to this man and told him that a start-up cola company called Pepsi was trying to gain a share of Coke's market by offering a 12-ounce bottle for 5 cents at a time when Coke was selling its famous 6-ounce bottle for the same price. Pepsi advertised "twice as much for a nickel too."[1] The marketing people suggested stopping this upstart in its tracks by putting Coke into a 12-ounce bottle like Pepsi. However, the future Coke chairman supposedly held up the 6-ounce bottle and said, "This bottle is our symbol, and we won't change it. This new cola company will fail like the numerous ones that tried to compete with us before."

When I was with Coke in the 1960s we were launching Tab for the new diet soda market. This same person—by now the chairman—watched impatiently as initial sales were sluggish and became very upset at the management team for championing the product. Eventually he fired most of the executive team from the president on down. Fortunately, old age finally forced the chairman to step down. Of course as Coke sales continually grew during his reign, the public saw Coke as a progressive, well-managed company under his leadership. Those on the inside knew otherwise.

Structural Unresponsiveness

The AFEs in American industry are so entrenched that their behemothlike structures are unresponsive even when presented with an opportunity. I consulted with a giant diversified chemical company whose business had been built on a synthetic fabric breakthrough 20 years earlier. Now management was looking for ways to get more out of its massive and expensive R&D effort. I interviewed a staff scientist who told me his work involved ways to force molecules together to make them even more compact. I asked if there was any practical application for his work. He thought for a moment and said, "I guess I could develop a lightweight cloth that could stop bullets." I was the first person to ask him about the commercial potential of his work. But more tragic was that nothing would be done about it because there was no mechanism to harvest the idea and profit from it. It just didn't fit into any of the company's mature business groups. The legacy of the structurally unresponsive AFEs is that manufacturing and process industries didn't develop and incubate new products in the 1970s to help them and the United States in the 1990s.

HOW TO MAKE YOUR BUSINESS MORE RESPONSIVE

Install a Forward-End-of-the-Business (FEB) Group

After years of consulting, I've come to the conclusion that most managers are quite capable of short-term operational thinking, and they gravitate toward day-to-day problem solving. As a result, in each company you can find only a few long-range or strategic thinkers. The lack of strategic thinking, as we have seen, is a major reason why the economy is in so much trouble. FEB is a matrix organization design developed by Ken Colmen and others at SRI that combines the strategic groups and individuals within a company who will be the sharp eyes that scan the horizon to identify opportunities and avoid unpleasant surprises. The FEB group would include the chief executive officer but not the chief operating officer whose responsibilities would be the day-to-day operations.

Also included should be representatives from New Business Development/Acquisitions, Research and Development, Strategic Planning, Government Affairs, Market Planning, and others who are responsible for providing a strategic road map for guiding the company through the mine fields of the 1990s.

Get Some Forward Thinkers on the Board

Just as we need to identify strategic thinkers within an organization, we must also broaden the vista of the board of directors. While leading a study to identify a new business area for a major toy manufacturer to enter through acquisition, my SRI team identified and sifted through over 100 candidates to identify 4 that fit all the criteria. These were presented to the board for review and all were rejected. Since that time, however, all of these opportunities, such as software, have developed into major business segments. As I presented each opportunity I was keenly aware how alien these businesses were to the board members, some of whom were running their own manufacturing businesses. And I should have realized the enormity of the gap that I had unsuccessfully tried to bridge in a single meeting. Although the strategic planning criteria allowed for a wide range of options, it was clear that the comfort level of the board did not.

In the 1990s, good opportunities will be rare. Boards must be familiar with innovation process. Their role should be to encourage innovation rather than shoot holes in the unfamiliar. Therefore, I strongly recommend having generalists such as FEB members, venture capitalists and management consultants on the boards to balance the members whose focus is limited to a specialized industry.

Become What Tom Peters Calls "A High-IQ Organization"[2]

I [Tom Peters] recently chatted with Dick Cavanagh, executive dean at Harvard's Kennedy School of Government, who coauthored *The Winning Performance: How America's High-Growth Midsize Companies Succeed.* He commented that the midsized stars outsmart rather than outslug the competition. '[They] live by their wits,' he says. I heard another twist on this theme in a speech by Japanese consultant Kenichi Ohmae. He described emerging 'brain-based models' of successful organizations that dominate greater Tokyo, Switzerland, Singapore, and Taiwan.

"The age of wits and brains also is the subject of British consultant Charles Handy's thought-provoking book, *The Age of Unreason.* Handy deduces the attributes of tomorrow's successful organization: 'For Britain and the rest of the industrialized world, it has to be brains. Clever people, making clever things or providing clever services add value, sometimes a lot of value, to minimal amounts of raw material. The degree of affluence may increase or wane in each country but labor-intensive manufacturing will not return to Europe, or to the USA and Japan.'

"Handy calls the brain-based species a 'shamrock organization.' It is 'based around a core of essential executives and workers (one leaf of the shamrock) supported by outside contractors (the second leaf).' He points out that this is 'not a new way of organizing things—builders large and small have operated this way for generations, as have newspapers with their printers and their stringers, or farmers with contract harvesting and holi-

day labor. What is new is the growth of this way of organizing in the big businesses and in the institutions in
the public sector. All organizations will soon become
shamrock organizations.'

"The tiny core group 'owns the knowledge,' Handy
says, and its central task is manipulating that knowledge to create new products and markets. But he emphasizes that the subsidiary part-time work and
subcontracting are not, as is often assumed, second-rate
pursuits. For instance, he cites a 1987 study that found
one-fifth of all "home workers" in Great Britain rank in
the top 10 percent in pay.

"Handy describes a prototypical organization: 'Walter
runs a design and consultancy business with a staff of
around 100 professionals . . . from a converted warehouse,
except that he hasn't converted it very much. There are no
offices in it. There are meeting rooms, a superb farm-house
kitchen, drawing boards scattered all around, word-proces-
sors, telephones and computers abounding . . . but no one,
not even Walter himself, has any private space—except for
the secretaries, who are really not secretaries but project
coordinators . . . . Walter told me, "[I want my consultants
and designers] with the client or working at home, where I
will provide any equipment they want. They only come in
here for meetings, to use some specialist equipment and,
generally, to keep in touch.'

"Handy offers another brain-based model, which he
calls the 'federal organization.' Just as our states
granted limited powers through the U.S. Constitution to
the central government, in Handy's federal model, 'the
initiative, the drive and the energy come mostly from the
bits, with the center of influencing force, relatively low
in profile.' Handy cites as an example the highly re-
garded Hanson organization. The $12.5 billion British
firm thrives with bare-bones staffing at the center. After
Hanson buys a company, it quickly pushes the acquisition to slash overhead and get closer to the customer—

major incentives for doing so are immediately put into place.

"Handy also explores work in the new organizations. It won't be placid or prescribed. Everyone will be 'expected not only to do all that is required but in some way to improve on that, to make a difference . . .'. Accordingly, Handy lays out a new career path: 'What does a career mean if it isn't always upwards? . . . The Japanese have a nice way of developing their high-potential young people. They actually have a fast-track up through the organization, it is a horizontal fast-track, a succession of . . . real jobs with tough standard to be met, but all at the same level.'

"Examples of the organizational forms that Handy describes are springing up in the United States—and are the thrust of many corporate restructurings. Just a decade ago, two-thirds of giant Monsanto's revenue came from commodity chemicals. Today, only 3 percent of its business is commodities. The rest is best described as 'customized' products—brain-based, that is. Another superb U.S. example is telecommunications upstart MCI. Unlike rival AT&T with its huge manufacturing arm, MCI takes pride in *not* manufacturing anything. MCI's business is knowledge; it adds value by integrating the work of others—its hundreds of sophisticated vendors.

"Handy's tract is revolutionary, yet it describes what's already happening at the leading edge of all developed economies. Read Handy. Better yet, ingest Handy. This is the shape of the future, uncomfortable and unfamiliar though it may be. If you are not moving quickly down the path suggested by Charles Handy—and being executed by the likes of Hanson—you are in danger of being scratched from the competitive race in the 1990s."

Have an Idea Search

One significant idea can change the direction of an individual or company. Think of how the idea "twice as much for a nickel too" changed the future from failure to success for Pepsi. While at SRI, I traveled the world as part of Joseph McPherson's Innovation Search Program, assisting organizations looking for significant new ideas. Conducting these week-long searches over the years, the team learned much about how to get people to generate ideas as well as how they kill ideas.

Table 7-1 is a list of some of the phrases that kill ideas around the world.

APPLYING CREATIVITY TECHNIQUES

The appendix contains some thoughts to consider when applying creativity techniques in organizations put together by Joe Grippo, a former innovation search team member. Conduct your own search for the winning ideas for the 1990s. I recommend it as a very worthwhile activity.

Increase Interaction

Increased interaction among R&D, marketing, production, and the customer can identify new opportunities, solidify relationships, and provide real-world insights for your business decisions. Key executives of major corporations must get out into the trenches. They frequently have little feel for their customers' needs and how the continuing economic hard times will affect purchasing decisions.

Have an "Incubator Businesses" Unit or Other Home for New Ideas

Have a home in your organization for new businesses or ideas that have come out of R&D or elsewhere but have not as yet been commercialized and do not fit into the existing organization structure. The "business incubator" allows new businesses the flexibility to test various

TABLE 7-1 Phrases That Kill Ideas Around the World

"It's against company policy."

"Top management would never go for it."

"That's beyond our responsibility."

"Has anyone else tried it?"

"That has already been tried in..."

"It won't work in our industry."

"No one would ever accept that."

"It's not feasible."

"It would be too expensive."

"Let's hold it in abeyance."

"It would be too impractical."

"We're not quite ready for that."

"It was tried years ago and..."

"It's not new; it reminds me of..."

"That would never work because..."

"I remember reading something like that."

"But what would you do about..."

"I considered that myself once, but..."

"It's great but ahead of its time."

"We've never done it that way before."

"But it would make our other products obsolete."

Finland: "Have they tried it in Sweden?"

In England: "Has ICI tried it yet?"

In Japan: "Where are the case studies?"

In the U.S.: "Put it down on one sheet of paper."

THE UNIVERSAL IDEA KILLER...
Silence.

SOURCE: Dr. Joseph McPherson.

product formats and markets without being penalized by the bottom-line orientation and rigid policy structures of established businesses units. A difficulty with the concept arises when the "product champion," who is often the developer of the idea, doesn't want to give up control of young business to those people assigned to make it grow.

I led several studies on how to develop industrial research parks for various foreign governments who wanted to develop their own Silicon Valley. In each case I recommended providing inexpensive, flexible space with shared core facilities to attract these incubator and start-up operations. I work two blocks away from the garage where Hewlett-Packard began. The synergies among the various companies like HP, universities, and research organizations in the many research parks in Northern California has bred numerous new businesses and products.

Develop the Qualities a Manager Needs in the Econoquake

The econoquake is a highly uncertain environment where there is a high potential for unpleasant surprises. A successful econoquake manager should aim for safety, flexibility, and maximizing options. Managers have to be prepared to be responsive to strategic and structural shifts.

THREE ECONOQUAKE MANAGERS SPEAK

Jim Rosen, Fantastic Foods

Jim Rosen is President of Fantastic Foods, a company whose sales have been growing steadily during these rough times. I asked Rosen what his strategic concerns were for the econoquake scenario.

He said, "There are three key questions in the strategic planning process for any business: How will you fare when the economy turns sour? How can you posture yourself to do well when that happens? And what changes will take place in the patterns of our consumers that we need to address? Obviously this is a more difficult issue for an auto manufacturer than for a food producer. People can put off buying a car but they won't put off eating their next meal. In fact, I believe that food becomes a growth industry in times of recession. People turn to food for consolation, for "simple pleasures," and perhaps for the "exciting adventure" that they cannot otherwise afford. Eating out a few extra times a month provides welcome recreation at a fraction of the price of a trip to Europe or a Caribbean cruise. People also tend to become more health conscious, which presents opportunities to non-traditional food entrepreneurs.

"We address these tendencies when we develop and position our products. We look at the long-term trends not only in food preferences, but in overall lifestyle. The erosion of purchasing power in our country began long before this particular recession and will continue into the next century. Our products must speak to the new constricted lifestyle.

"Good business practices work in good times and bad. Produce a high-quality product. Aggressively become a leader in your category. Treat people like people. And always keep from getting 'fat' and wasteful as a company. The boy who has lots of experience swimming won't drown when you throw him in the water. Perhaps we should operate as though there is always a recession going on."

Gene Biggi, Beaverton Foods

Beaverton Foods of Beaverton, Oregon, the world's largest producer of sweet mustards, has also been growing steadily during a very difficult market. I asked Gene

Biggi, Beaverton's president, to share his formula for success in today's difficult market.

Work Out Your Problems on the Road Before Opening on Broadway. First and most important, Beaverton Foods did its homework to establish this company many years ago. "I started slowly in Idaho, Montana, Washington and Oregon, which were relatively easy markets to establish our product lines in. Customers in these markets are more faithful to local brands, rather than national brands. This was especially true 20 or 30 years ago. My long-range plan was to do my homework and work out all the problems before I moved to California, Chicago, etc. Hard work and research to develop the right package helped."

Don't Go One-on-One Against a Tank. "I tried never to compete with national companies. We concentrated on improving our product line and developing specialty condiments that larger companies had no interest in producing. Offer quality, price, and service. Foreign companies had the specialty market pretty much to their own; however, their products were not of high quality and were overpriced. Our main product 35 years ago was horseradish, and then I began to develop a specialty mustard line which no one else had. I added special import items, and produced and distributed with this line. We offered a better product, better service, at better prices. It took many years to earn the respect of the specialty food distributors, I backed them up 100% with quality and service."

Build a Lock on a Niche. "Today, Beaverton Foods is in a positive position because of hard work years ago. We're big enough that large national companies can't penetrate our business and they can't produce our type of products. When smaller companies try to duplicate, they don't have the expertise or the financial backing that is required, therefore they can't do well and don't have a chance of success on a national basis."

Be Conservative with Money. "Beaverton Foods has also been a conservative company. We have only expanded when we had cash to broaden our markets. All available monies were used to invest in new manufacturing equipment and product development. All expansion was done on a cash basis."

Have a Responsive Branding Strategy. "Also a great deal of success for Beaverton comes from the fact that we can survive the retail trade with three different brands. Beaver Brand mostly goes to the supermarket trade. It has preservatives and a long shelf-life—one to two years. Old Spice Gold sells in upgrade supermarkets, specialty stores, delis and department stores. That line contains no preservatives. Inglehoffer is a unique bowl-type jar found in all areas of stores, as well as in delis and in gift packs."

Be Responsive in Product Development. "Lastly, the main success of our company is quality. Each day throughout the year we concentrate on at least 1 of our over 150 formulas. We are constantly trying to improve the flavor and extend shelf life. Larger companies aren't able to accomplish this type of product development. Once they have a product available on a national basis, it's almost impossible to change a formula."

Jack Painter, ADM (Archer Daniels Midland Company)

Marketing and Selling in the 1990s. Tough Times Ahead? ADM's marketing director, Jack Painter says, "All of us in the business have a tendency to worry and fret as we look at what's ahead of us...as we close out the 20th century.

"All we hear is:

Consumers are cutting back.

We are in a recession.

There is a proliferation of new products.

Product labeling needs to be revised.

Consumer needs are changing.

Population is aging and not growing,

And so on and so on.

"All of these types of influences are probably not much different from the *types* of influences that have existed in past decades. I think that to be successful in both marketing and selling, one has to get back to the basics—such things as meeting consumer and customer needs and not just corporate needs; good value for a fair price; new and unique items and services, and not just the same old 'Me, too' type products, programs and promotions we see all the time. Once we're sure that we meet these attributes, then we must aggressively sell to both consumers and customers and not be willing to settle for anything less than the results we expect. The old phrase, 'good enough is never good enough,' certainly applies as we face the remainder of the decade. Insurmountable challenges? No, just a different version of what we have always faced and, I might add, have been successful at overcoming. Is there growth ahead? You bet, and those who meet the challenges head on will be successful in the end."

Strategies to Prosper During the Econoquake

1. Redefine your Business for Additional Sales. Use a big-net business strategy in tough times and take a broader view of what your business is about. Gillette sold

razor blades for years before going into shaving cream.
Midas realized that while its workers were checking
your muffler they could also check your brakes. Supermarkets are selling nonprescription drugs, while drug-
stores are selling food. Don't place all your bets in one
place, because you could lose big. That was the problem
with banks. They bet too heavily on commercial real estate and got killed for it. What new product or service
can you be supplying? Who will be your customer in the
1990s?

2. Diversify or Sell Before Assets Disappear. If you
see your business declining, either sell your business or
try developing or acquiring another business before your
assets are drained. Why is Chrysler spending billions on
a new R&D facility when it has fallen out of the Big
Three automakers? Doesn't Chrysler management realize its most likely future scenario is decreasing market
share in a shrinking market? It would be better off using
its assets to buy its way into another industry with better growth potential in recessionary times. Do you see
the handwriting on the wall for your business? As a
business broker, I know how much easier it is to sell a
growing company than one whose sales have begun to
decline. Have updated financial and marketing prepared
for your review. If the direction of your business since
1990 is down, the econoquake is very likely to continue
that unfortunate trend.

3. Watch Out for Hot Growth Companies. Right now
biotechnology is hot, but its continued growth depends on
the federal government's willingness to continue funding
health care. When the econoquake hits, the government
will be cutting back on funding for everything, including
biotech. Business that would normally be the hot growth
companies of the 1990s will cool off quickly during the
econoquake. Look to businesses that deal in basics such as
food and fuel, things that people must have. Businesses

that meet demographic trends such as services for seniors will also do well.

4. Don't Count on the Export Market. As the econoquake spreads globally, even the strategy of depending on exports for diversification may not work. Most countries in the world will be in worse economic shape than we are. Focus your attention on the most profitable consumer market in the world—the United States.

5. Be a big Fish in a Small Pond. The best strategy may be survival in a small market, with few competitors. GE won't be in any market where it can't be number one or two. There are still many consumer niche markets such as outdoor furniture that are not controlled by giant corporations. My consulting practice has identified many others.

6. Small is O.K. Smaller companies have a better chance to survive the econoquake. The Asian model of small businesses with lower overhead and increased responsiveness has proven successful over long periods of tough economic times. Just look at the difficulty that our giant companies—IBM, Citibank, GM—are having. The most successful of our big companies are trying to make themselves smaller and leaner and more decentralized.

WAYS TO MAKE YOUR BUSINESS FIT AND LEAN

1. Cut Expenses Early in the Recession. Businesses tend to wait too long before making decisions that require disruption and change. If your assets are being drained by an extended period of poor sales while your fixed overhead remains high, make the tough decisions to scale down. Spend some time looking at ways to reduce your overhead, and compute the money you can save by taking action sooner rather than later. You know your business climate better than economists. If you sense long-term trouble, act accordingly, and don't be misled by talk of economic recovery.

2. Review How Your Organization is Structured to Cut Costs. A technique that often provides an opportunity to cut costs without reducing organizational effectiveness is to review your organization structure. As a company evolves over time, the logic for how its organization is structured no longer makes sense. An international food and beverage company needed a forecast of how many people and in what positions would be needed over a five-year period. When reviewing the organization chart, I noticed a number of administrative positions being duplicated in neighboring countries. When I asked about this, I was informed that when the business first evolved in each country, a separate administrative unit was set up. We recommended areawide administration in many regions as a way to reduce overhead. Look at your organizations to locate opportunities to combine departments and functions. In the 1980s the tendency was to add staff and departments that no longer can be supported in the 1990s. Let's face it: many organizations need belt tightening. There are few organizations where people are working at even 50% of their capacity. Unfortunately, there simply isn't enough work to keep them busy. Decide on a revised business strategy for the 1990s, and then select the organization structure that best supports those goals. Don't force fit an old structure to meet new objectives.

3. Be Aggressive about Accounts Receivable. Slow payments are an early sign of potential problems such as bankruptcy. The old saw, "The sale isn't made until the check clears the bank," is valid in these recessionary times. Therefore, don't pay sales commissions until you receive payment from the customer. Pick up overdue payments while making periodic visits to your customers. Ask for the check directly. Many people feel uncomfortable about asking for money. It's more difficult to make excuses such as "the check's in the mail" when you meet face to face. Have strict limits on how much merchandise you will sell on credit. Where there has been a past credit problem, ship only on a cash on delivery basis. Regularly check the financial status of your key customers through a credit reporting service.

4. Cut Marketing Expense Carefully. Review how you market your products in tough times. As people can't find work, large numbers of high quality talent become available for minimal cost. Consider developing a commission-only arrangement, and replace unproductive full-time sales people with aggressive independent rep organizations. The price of media to place your advertising will also come down. In tough times, don't stop your advertising and sales activities. Instead, become a tough negotiator and reduce expenses rather than marketing services.

5. Take Discounts on Accounts Payable. Rather than slowing payment on your bills, ask the vendor for a discount of 2% if you make payments within ten days. These discounts can yield big savings if taken on all purchases over time. If you must slow down payments due to cash flow problems, call your suppliers and let them know. Most suppliers will understand and work with you rather than risk losing a customer in a competitive market.

6. Cutting Medical Insurance Expense. Earl Dworkin, president of Dworkin Insurance Services, suggests the following action during the econoquake: Make the personal deductible higher so the monthly premium can be reduced. This holds true for group and individual insurance. Carve out children from a group plan under the age of 23 if they are in good health and put them on an individual youth care plan either with Blue Cross or Blue Shield. This will cut costs in half. Large group life (100 or more) could be self-funded by the employer. This could save the employer large amounts of money in out-of-pocket expenses if the total risk doesn't explode. The insurance carrier will assume the risk after the accumulative expenses reach a certain level.

7. Work Just-in-Time (JIT) on Inventories. U.S. business built up inventories when business was good or when they were offered a deal too good to refuse on needed supplies. During the econoquake, using the Japanese just-in-time inventory system can save big bucks. The system I watched work so successfully at the Mitsubishi car plant in Japan requires developing close links with your suppliers so that you can plan your supply and delivery needs together, thereby turning your inventory more often and reducing cash outlay as well as storage and handling costs. Also, return unused inventory to suppliers, sell excess finished products, and wholesale obsolete materials and products that are wasting space that you are paying for.

8. Refinance Debt. Take immediate advantage of the low interest rates to renegotiate existing bank loans. Bring up-to-date financial statements, including projections as well as other positive materials, that the loan officer can package for the bank's loan committee. Make sure your projections include enough surplus cash to cover the loans. Discuss how the loan will help grow the business rather than suggesting that you need the cash because the business is in trouble. Shop around for the best deal. There is nothing wrong with your telling the banker what you will think about the loan terms and get back to them shortly.

9. Consolidate Space or Relocate. With commercial real estate in trouble, now is a perfect time to speak to landlords about rent concessions. Landlords cannot afford to lose tenants when occupancies are low and their debt payments high.

CONSIDERATION BEFORE GOING INTO BUSINESS

1. Opportunities to Buy Businesses. As the economy worsens, there will be increasing opportunities to buy existing businesses at fire-sale prices. Large and small companies as well as divisions will be put on the selling block. Several large clients of mine have found that they can no longer afford the human and financial resources to grow businesses they acquired in the 1980s and have consolidated their strategic direction to only core business. Also, as older Americans are deciding to retire earlier, many small mom-and-pop businesses are coming on the market. Of course, many of these owners see a bleak future for their businesses and want to get out while they can. Unfortunately, those that don't sell quick enough will go under. There will be many good opportunities to pick up businesses' assets such as client lists, machinery, vehicles, inventory, and brand names before they go bankrupt.

2. Start Your Own Business. If your job prospects are poor, consider starting your own business. Even in good economic times, people want to be their own boss. Existing businesses are usually busy keeping existing customers happy and leave opportunity gaps for entrepreneurs with keen eyes on the market place. I've had the pleasure of assisting several start-up operations and watching them grow. In 1980, following up on an idea found in a book entitled *One Hundred Businesses You Can Start for $100.* Two enterprising Santa Cruz (California) musicians bought a few boxes of oranges and a used juicing machine and set up shop in their backyard.

They began delivering fresh squeezed juice to local restaurants. Today Odwalla employs 115 people, occupies
a 6,000-square foot facility, and services over 700 accounts.

**3. Develop a Strategic Marketing Plan for the
1990s.** Minkin Affiliates, my consulting firm, has developed a strategic market planning approach to prepare and position companies and products for the
tough times ahead. A company run by the new breed of
managers that is succeeding in 1990s, and which used
Minkin Affiliates' marketing model in the 1980s, is the
Odwalla Juice Company. Greg Steltenpohl, its socially
responsible president, agreed to share parts of this
plan.

Greg, one of the original Odwalla owners, was
aware the importance of strategic planning from the
earliest stages of the business. No matter how small
your business, take time to plan. In the 1990s your
business future depends on it. Using the greatly abbre-
viated business model presented here or your own
framework, set up a planning weekend. Review your
existing business or ideas for a new product or business by modifying this beverage example approach.
Remember, size has no relationship to the need to
think long term and strategically.

THE ECONO 2000 STRATEGIC
PLANNING MODEL

Figure 7-1 displays the Econo 2000 strategic planning
model.

Step 1. Highlight an Economic Scenario. You can assume the following economic scenario or if you're more optimistic, run one or two alternative scenarios or modify the
econoquake scenario.

FIGURE 7-1 Econo 2000 Strategic Market Planning Model

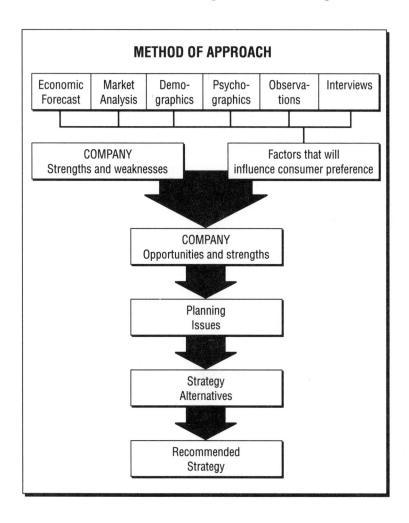

SOURCE: Minkin Affiliates

• Flat, then steadily declining economic growth; most sales growth through acquisition.

• Greater consolidation; few giant companies and increased number of very small companies.

• Declining profits in most businesses.

• Consumers have less disposable income.

• Large companies rule traditional distribution channels.

• Price becomes King.

• Growth of the underground cash market.

• Growth of factory outlet and warehouse operations.

• More products being offered by offshore producers.

What are the Implications of this Economic Scenario to Your Organization?

Step 2. Look at Your Particular Market Niche and Highlight its Key Trends. We found the beverage market, for example, to be a mature market controlled by population and consumption patterns. Distribution control and brand appeal are the keys. Startups and new concepts peak and shake out quickly—look what happened to wine coolers.

• Increase in private label products being produced by others.

• Restaurants had a limited selection of beverage choices.

• Promotion costs were increasing.

• Packaging preferences change by region of the country—for example, the south prefers juice in a can.

• Fewer supermarkets doing more volume.

- Many immigrant small store owners—an opportunity?

- Decline of small stores.

- People will buy in the same stores, but will buy less and be more selective.

- More competition, more awareness where the market is going.

What's Going to Happen to Your Market Niche Over the Next 3–5 Years?

Step 3. Demographic Trends that Will Affect Your Business.

- Growth of ethnic populations means food will be conservative and traditional for many.

- Eating out will continue—even the poor eat out.

- Regional differences and preferences: west more open to new products, southerners like their soft drinks.

- Grazing—continuous snacking over sitting down for a full meal—will continue.

- More men doing shopping.

- Living close to the edge, spending with no savings cushion.

- Food preparation time decreasing.

- Nutrition, being casual, nature and ecology important—serious consideration of price/value relationship.

What Demographic Trends Will Impact Your Market?

Step 4. Think Lifestyles. Develop a logic hook to view lifeways and styles of your customers. Minkin Affiliates uses a proprietary life style model ("light/dark psychographic") that relates food and beverage preference to age, lifestyle, and ethnicity.

Our "young light" Odwalla Juice drinker will, for example, also prefer salad, grains, health foods, will read labels, is price aware, doesn't want sugar or preservatives, likes demonstrations and logic, is college-educated, mobile, environmentally and socially concerned.

What Do You Know About the Lifestyle of Your Customers? What Implications are There for What Products You Sell and How You Market?

Step 5. Get Out Into the Field and Observe and Interview Your Customers. I employ a small-sample observational approach that has given considerable insights into customers needs and buying behavior. The approach is to have my affiliates observe how people shop, ask questions and take notes on their behavior. We then compare notes and look for similarities and differences in the observed behaviors. In the Odwalla project, some of the observations were that people in the "young dark" segment expected and preferred orange juice to be yellow in color not orange. Also noted:

- The importance of carrot juice to the health conscious light segments of the psychographic.

- Price not a factor for small single service sizes.

Do You Take Time to Observe Your Customers?

When was the last time you asked your customers about your product, your competition, and what they would like in a new product or a modification of an existing one?

Step 6. Combine the Inputs from Steps 1 Through 5 and Develop an Extensive List of the Factors that Will Influence the Buying Behavior of Your Customer.

Step 7. Develop a List of Your Company's Strengths and Weaknesses.

- Strengths: Satisfaction among regular users; perception of quality; harmonious labor environment; products in sync with or ahead of lifestyles.

- Weaknesses: Difficult product from a perishability and handling standpoint; lack of advertising.

Step 8. Develop a list of opportunities and threats.

- Opportunities: Supermarket expansion; food service; develop new products.

- Threats: Loss of supply; loss of facility; loss of key employees; increased competition.

Step 9. Develop Planning Issues. Planning issues are the key concerns you must address in any market strategy.

- How to pace production with growth.

- How to finance expansion.

- How to assure supply.

- How to expand marketing/sales efforts.

Step 10. Develop Strategic Alternatives that Solve the Planning Issues Raised in step 9.

- Acquire a company with distribution beyond Northern California.

- Develop an additional facility for production.

- Use a distributor outside the area.
- Employ all of the above.

Step 11. Recommend a Strategy and Implement.

CONSIDER PRODUCTS OR SERVICES FOR THE FOLLOWING 25 INDUSTRIES WHICH WILL CONTINUE TO DO WELL IN TROUBLED TIMES

Security

Funeral parlors

Nursing homes

Food

Beverages

Drugs

Greeting cards

Florists

Plumbers

Auto mechanics

Health care

Household products

Telephone companies

Gas, electric, and water utilities

Waste disposal

Privately run prisons

Health insurance

Marriage and family counseling

Financial planners

Fast-food restaurants

Factory outlets

Entertainment, e.g., movies, videos

Health clubs

Travel

Shoe repair

OTHER BUSINESS TRENDS TO BE AWARE OF IN THE 1990s

1. Government on Your Back. Why anyone would want to start a business in this environment is still somewhat puzzling given the nightmare of having to deal with government laws and regulations that allow the United States to support 70% of the world's lawyers. Expect more of the same. How about the recent access for the handicapped regulations for a can of worms? The confusion and the no-win nature of the legislation will continue to keep lawyers busy. Large cash settlements to criminals who claim mistreatment and homeless who smell up a library will encourage frivolous lawsuits that the public ends up paying for with increased fees and taxes.

2. The Niche Grab. Companies will move to capture niche markets. Semiconductor companies will try to move from the mass markets to the custom chip markets. This will require major production changes. The acquisition business is looking at smaller opportunities with growth potential to capture control of niche markets.

3. More Protectionism. Expect more protectionist legislation in the United States and around the world as economic conditions continue to decline. In Los Angeles a major railway car deal won by the Japanese was overturned in this buy-American climate and given to a U.S. company.

4. The Japanese will Buy Elsewhere. The Japanese will slow their investment activity in the United States for several reasons. There are faster growing world markets such as Germany and the newly industrialized countries of South East Asia, and the rise in the value of the dollar against the yen reduces the value of the properties bought by the Japanese in the United States. Unless the trend is reversed, expect the Japanese quietly to begin selling many properties. These will provide many investment opportunities.

5. Growth of the International Market Place. Many countries are depending on the U.S. market for their exports. The infusion of foreign products will give an international bazaar flavor to retail shops, department stores, and particularly clothing and food stores. Much of the clothing we wear is already manufactured overseas. These foreign producers will need help in understanding the U.S. market. While I was at SRI, a Japanese company with a very popular fermented milk product sold in Japan wanted to sell its product in the United States. My first suggestion after biting my tongue was that they change the name from "Calpis" to something else, but not to "Pocari Sweat," another popular Japanese beverage. My daughter, who teaches English in Japan, finds that anything with English writing on it sells well in Japan even if the writing doesn't make much sense in English. Sweatshirts with fractured English phases and cars sporting chrome letters spelling out "Saloon" are examples of a new language.

In simpler times, a fully equipped "tool kit" contained relatively few tools. And those sufficed to do the job—whatever the job—for a relatively long time. For millenia, tools had a very long lifespan of usefulness. Fast forwarding, we realize that only a century ago, tools were still being passed from father to son, for several generations.

Times have changed and the speed of change has quickened enormously. As has been suggested in this chapter, the "tools" now required to keep up to date—and stay in business—include long-range vision, forward-thinking, the embracing of innovation, and a "tool kit" crammed with every device or strategy that can give them an edge. Businesses no longer have the leisure to correct mistakes. Today, there is no room for error, no time for hesitation. The next generation of business people will have to be the best ever.

ENDNOTES

1. Lyrics from "Pepsi-Cola Radio Jingle" © Pepsi Co., Inc., 1940.

2. Reprinted with permission from Tom Peter's syndicated newspaper column.

INVESTING
DURING
THE ECONOQUAKE

There is no such thing as "zero risk."
William Driver

Take calculated risks. That is quite different from being rash.
General George Smith Patton

During the first period of a man's life the greatest danger is: not to take risks.
Sören Kierkegaard

A pinch of probability is worth a pound of perhaps.
James Thurber

Be wary of the man who urges action in which he himself incurs no risk.
Joaquin Setanti

When economic times are good, it's easy to decide where to invest your money. Almost every investment will rise in value. In a depression, the opportunities are more limited, and the choices you make are critical to your economic well-being. This chapter presents an investment program that can help you invest wisely even though the 1990s promises to be a period of great uncertainty and economic troubles.

The following 13 guidelines will provide a solid basis for making good money in troubled times.

LIQUIDATE ASSETS NOW

To prosper during the econoquake, you must have cash to take advantage of investment opportunities as they come along. During the early phases of the econoquake, people are confused by the mixed signals the economy and the economists are giving out. They hear about the beginning of the recovery or that the 1990s are going to be boom times. Hearing this sort of talk, many people fail to take the possibility of a depression seriously. However, the perceptive few will see that a depression is inevitable. Those who possess the wisdom and courage to act on their insight will be the ones who prosper.

What will happen? More layoffs and corporate bankruptcies will occur as the econoquake unfolds. Taken together, this means that the level of risk is incredibly high. Eventually, many people will find themselves holding worthless investments or will need to cash in their investments because they've lost their jobs.

As the econoquake progresses, the value of many of the assets you own will decrease in value. Most assets grew in the 1980s but most will continually decrease in value in the 1990s. To safeguard the value of your assets, sell them during the early stages of the econoquake. Liquidate at once all assets that are not providing you a source of income.

How do you go about this? Make a list of your assets and put a checkmark next to those that are essential to keep and those that you can sell. Actively try to sell assets such as real estate, art and other collections, gold jewelry, coins, and other precious metals. Selling real estate demands some careful considerations. If the location is prime, consider holding onto real estate. Don't forget excess furniture, appliances, and power tools.

The price of assets will continually decline as the depression deepens. As more and more assets put up for sale compete in a tight-money environment, prices will decline, plummeting prices to pre-1980 levels during the deflationary phase of the depression.

HAVE SIX MONTHS OF LIVING EXPENSE IN A MONEY MARKET OR SAVINGS ACCOUNT

The proverbial "rainy day" is about to arrive. Have you been saving for it? If you are like most people, your savings has been declining over the last few years because you haven't been placing part of your earnings into savings on a regular basis. On average, Americans save only about 5% of their pretax earnings as compared to over 25% by the Japanese. Now is the time to get serious about building a savings cushion. In fact, such a cushion is critical. In good economic times, a savings cushion of three months is sufficient, but with a major depression about to hit, a minimum of six months' reserves for living expenses is a must.

A savings cushion allows you some choice in making important life decisions. Like opting for survival! There will be a growing wave of permanent layoffs. If you are laid off, how will you and your family cope while you look for work? In good times, a job search can typically take six months for an executive position, and when times are bad and so many are competing for jobs, it can take far longer. Without a savings cushion, you may be forced to accept a position that isn't right for you. You may be forced to move or sell assets at a loss. It is difficult to make the decisions if you act out of panic rather than according to logic.

SAVE!

"But after I pay my bills, there's no money left at the end of the month." This is what I usually hear from clients and friends, no matter how much income they have. Let's review some basic savings tips:

- *Small amounts saved regularly add up.* I think of going back East to visit my mother after my father passed away several years ago. She asked my help with sorting out their business affairs. While going through her shoe box files, I came across one of Mom's savings passbooks that showed a balance of several thousand dollars. Knowing how she scrimped to feed and clothe three sons and that her only employment was as a nursery school aide and baby sitter, I asked her about this savings account. She smiled at my surprise and shared her savings tips.

- *Put something away from each payment received,* no matter how small it was. *Live within a budget* to assure that savings are not withdrawn. This allows interest to compound, giving you interest on interest. Typical of their generation, my parents had learned the importance of a savings cushion from the hard real-world lessons taught in the Great Depression. Later generations that have not experienced the depression not only don't save, they continue to spend and to borrow to do so.

Some Tips My Mother Didn't Tell Me

Here are some more good suggestions:

Reward Yourself. To save money, you must cut expenses or increase income. Both seem to be painful alternatives and are generally avoided. A psychological tool that helps people undertake something unpleasant is to promise—and deliver—something pleasurable upon its completion. Therefore, reward yourself when you defer a major expenditure or reach a savings goal.

Make Savings Automatic.

- *Write a check to savings.* Another savings suggestion is to write a check for savings when you pay your monthly bills or have money automatically deducted from payroll and placed into a savings account.

- *"Keep the change."* You might as well keep it yourself! Have a place to put the change left in your pockets or purse at the end of each day.

- *Make stocks really pay.* Reinvest stock dividends instead of cashing them in and spending the proceeds.

REDUCE DEBT

To have more income to invest, reduce your debt. Servicing debt is very expensive. It's also a poor investment. In considering how to reduce debt, look at the two kinds of expenses you probably have:

> Fixed expenses remain the same each month. Fixed expenses include rent or mortgage payments, taxes, loan payments, and insurance premiums.

> Variable expenses dependent on outside circumstances or our actions. Variable expenses include entertainment, telephone bills, food, and travel.

We miss opportunities to reduce our debt if we think of fixed expense as expenses beyond our control. These expenses are really "fixed" because our thinking about them is fixed.

I hear people wail, "I'm stuck with these expenses; I have to live!" But to survive, circumstances may demand that we change how we live.

Let's look at typical expenses. You'll be surprised at how many ways you can reduce them.

Pay Off Credit Card Balances. In these times of low money market interest, reduce monthly expense by paying off credit card balances that often charge double-digit interest. It makes more sense to pay off an auto loan charging 13% interest than to purchase a $15,000 certificate of deposit earning only 6.5%.

Be Very Selective When Borrowing. Borrow for certain long-term investments that seem sensible but not for luxury items. Current low interest rates make a 30-year fixed mortgage a great deal if you want to own a home.

Avoid Lending. Don't lend money in troubled times unless you can afford not to get it back. After all, you don't want to find yourself needing a loan.

Become a Savvy Shopper. Become a better purchaser. You can save large quantities of cash by shopping wisely. Areas that especially reward the smart shopper are insurance, including life, health, disability, homeowner, and auto.

Trim Expenses. Do your own laundry, eat at home, skip the movies and rent a video instead, collect and use coupons. Cut down on long-distance calls; have the phone company evaluate your calling pattern and recommend the most efficient plan for your usage. Shut your appliances, lights, and computer off when they're not in use. Turn down heat and air conditioning. Cancel magazine subscriptions. Plan your food menus to take advantage of "specials" and leftovers. Eat more fruit and vegetables; they're not only healthier for you, they're cheaper.

It all adds up. If most weeks you eat in when you'd eat out, rent a video instead of seeing a movie, and press your own shirt you will save about $1,000 in one year.

BE CAREFUL WHERE YOU KEEP YOUR CASH

Banks are not the safe places for your money that they used to be. Remember, if there were to be a run on the banks, the Federal Deposit Insurance Corporation (FDIC) insurance would only cover a small percentage of depositors. During the econoquake there will be more bank failures and consolidations. Therefore, it's prudent to be cautious about where you keep your money.

The goal of the FDIC is to avoid banking panic, not to pay out. It has very limited reserves in case of massive bank failures. When a bank is in trouble, the government seizes the bank and attempts to look for a buyer. If one can't be found, the FDIC will pay out up to $100,000 per account, but there is no fixed timetable as to when depositors will actually receive their money. New owners of the failed bank are not obligated to existing interest rates or lines of credit. As the number of bank failures increase during the econoquake, the FDIC's limited reserves will run out, and politicians are becoming increasingly skittish about bank bailouts.

Here are some guidelines to help safeguard your nest egg.

Don't Put All Your Eggs in One Basket. Select a financial professional to recommend at least two banks with a solid foundation. Keep your money in at least two different banks.

Save in the Best Banks. Go to your local library and check *Moody's* and *Standard & Poor's* for listings of the highest-rated banks in your area.

Read the Fine Print. During the econoquake, make sure you read the fine print on loan applications. Many have an "at-risk" clause that allows the bank to call in your loan if the bank is in extreme trouble. Work with banks that don't have such clauses or will delete them.

THE TWO-PART INVESTMENT PROTFOLIO

Think of your investment portfolio as having two parts. The first part should contain investments that are "Safety first," low-risk, short-term, fixed-rate-of-return debt investments. This will assure that your nest egg doesn't crack during an adverse economic scenario. It will also provide guaranteed returns. This kind of investment includes certificates of deposit, money market funds, passbook savings accounts, and debt-based mutual funds, bonds, and notes.

The second part of your investment portfolio should offer growth opportunities; such opportunities entail risk. Examples include moderate- and high-risk equity investments that offer greater potential growth over an undetermined time horizon. Equity investments include stocks, equity-based mutual funds, and real estate.

To prosper during the econoquake, you need a strategy that mixes the two parts of the portfolio to meet individualized amounts of desirable risk and income.

Part One of Your Portfolio: Safety-First, Short-Term Debt Investments

The investment strategy for retirees or anyone else who wants low risk is clear. They will just have to accept very low returns by putting their money into government securities, and the sooner the better. Right now, many retirees, traumatized by the low yields on certificates of deposit (CDs), are chasing higher returns in the bond and stock market. These people can get burned.

Don't use the safety part of your portfolio for anything risky.

Let's review the kinds of investments that can help keep you safe.

Certificates of Deposit. If you don't have more than six months' cash reserve for living expenses, stay liquid and put your money in financial instruments that mature in less than one year. CDs, money market mutual funds, and Treasury issues are good choices. CDs commonly mature at three and six months and can be bought for $500 or less. They are fixed rate investments, and the rate of interest increases with the length of the term of the investment.

Interest rates vary, so do some comparison shopping. Most CDs are insured by the FDIC for up to $100,000 and so are safe choices. But do not put more than $100,000 in a single account, since, as explained earlier, individual accounts are government insured for a maximum of $100,000.

Money Market Mutual Funds. Mutual funds pool money from many investors and are invested under professional management in the sale and purchase of short-term financial instruments. They are sold by mutual funds and stockbrokers. The pooling allows investors with as little as $1,000 to invest to take advantage of high interest previously reserved for people with $100,000 to invest. These fund investments include commercial paper from top-rated corporations, jumbo bank CDs, and government securities, such as Treasury bills and government agency debt. These usually safe, high-quality instruments mature in 30 to 90 days. They are very liquid, which means that you can exchange them for cash within a day or two. Most of these funds also give you limited check-writing privileges of $500 or more. There is no cost to put money into a money market mutual fund or to take money out, and your return compounds daily.

This sounds good, doesn't it? However, money market mutual funds are not insured by the FDIC. Moreover, the econoquake greatly increases the chances that corporations issuing commercial paper may default. Therefore, look at funds that have a high percentage of their assets in government securities such as Treasury bills. The yield from these funds is generally a little less, but the peace of mind is worth the difference. If you choose funds with commercial paper, check the prospectus to be sure most of the corporations are in depressionproof businesses like food and the others listed in Chapter 7.

Treasury Issues. Remember, only the government can print money when it needs it. Therefore, these instruments are the safest way to keep your cash. They come in three forms:

Treasury bills are short-term government paper with no stated interest rate. They are sold at a discount through competitive bidding and reach maturity in 90 days or less. You might prefer to buy your T-bills directly from Federal Reserve banks rather than stockbrokers to avoid paying a fee.

Treasury bonds are U.S. government bonds issued in units of $1,000.00, with maturities of five years or longer. They are traded on the market like other bonds.

Treasury notes are U.S. government paper that mature in one to ten years and pay out at a fixed rate of interest twice a year. The minimum investment is $1,000 for notes maturing in four years or more and $5,000 for those maturing in less than four years.

Bank Savings Account. Again, there are pluses and minuses. Your bank savings account is liquid—you can make withdrawals and deposits at will—but the interest you receive from this kind of account is very low. Your accounts are FDIC insured, but CDs, which are also insured, pay higher interest rates.

If you don't have money in a savings and loan, don't put any in. If you have money in a savings and loan, make sure it's insured by the Savings Association Insurance Fund (SAIF), which guaranties deposits up to $100,000.

If you have money in a credit union, make sure it's federally funded and that its accounts are insured up to $100,000 through the National Credit Union Share Insurance Fund.

Bank Money Market Accounts.   These money market accounts, which are sold at banks, credit unions, and savings and loans, are federally insured. These bank certificates pay more than the passport savings rate but carry some penalty for early withdrawal.

Checking Accounts.   Checking accounts have guaranteed liquidity but pay interest only if you keep a sizable balance. Checking accounts are for paying out money—paying your bills; they are not a good instrument for making money.

Part Two of Your Portfolio: Moderate- to High-Risk Investments

The more you look to investments to provide financial growth, the more risk comes with the opportunity. Let's look at typical moderate- to high-risk investments, common and preferred stocks and bonds.

Common Stocks.   All corporations issue common stock and sell stock shares as a way to raise capital. When you buy one of these shares, you become a shareholder, or part owner, in the corporation. The advantage of equity investments such as stock is that there is no limit on how high the value of your investment can grow. You

could make a bundle! Many have. The disadvantage of
stocks, however, is that they offer no guaranteed principal or rate of return.

Stock is sold to the public in two stages. Shares are
first sold in what is called an initial public offering
(IPO). The purchasers of IPOs constitute the primary
market for stocks. Shares are then sold to other investors through the stock exchanges—the secondary market.

A stock's price at a given time is determined by the
amount people are willing to pay to buy the stock and
the price at which people will sell their shares.

Dividends are paid by some companies out of profits. Companies that pay out high dividends are called
"income stocks." Utility stocks fit into this category.
Other companies plow their earnings back into their
businesses and pay no dividends in expectation that
"growing the business" will increase their share price,
making them a worthwhile investment. These are called
"growth stocks."

The yield for a stock is the relationship between the
dividend paid by the stock and its market price. At any
given time, the dividend received is the same per share.
However, the price paid for the shares may vary. If you
paid $100.00 for a stock and the dividend is $2.00, your
original yield is 2%; if you bought the stock at $50.00,
your yield was 4%. Obviously, we all want to buy low
and sell high to get a big yield. But since everyone wants
to do this, actually doing it is far from a cinch. People
most likely to achieve big yields are knowledgeable
about the behavior of the stock market.

Preferred Stocks. These equities are senior, or "preferred," only in that they have a dividend preference
over common stocks. This means that holders of these
stocks must be paid dividends before common shareholders receive dividends. Some preferred stocks are convertible to common stock; such stocks have a "conversion

ratio" that is used to determine precisely how they are converted. Owing to the market price premium that is paid for high-yielding preferred stock, A-rated corporate bonds that pay higher rates of return are often more attractive to investors.

Playing the Market

One thing that is certain during the 1990s is that the investment climate will fluctuate wildly. Therefore, do not risk your short-term safety funds in the stock market in hopes of capturing fast profits. You could win—but losing would be too painful. Instead, keep safety funds in cash or cash equivalents, discussed in the safety-first section of your investment portfolio.

The stock market is not necessarily connected with economic reality. In mid-1992, for example, the market registered a record high while the economic outlook is for a long-term depression.

Speculating in this market is all too much like gambling in a casino, and the results of doing so are also likely to be similar. In dangerous times, gambling isn't a good idea; planning and carrying out a sound investment strategy is what's needed. The market will also mislead those people who view it as an indicator that typically turns up six months ahead of the economy.

Econoquake Slippery Slope Theory. If, as I believe, the econoquake has begun to surface and will soon plunge the economy into a major depression, companies with declining sales in this early stage of the depression will have very little chance of recovery as the depression deepens. Check to see if your stock pick has started down the slippery slope by tracking actual sales. On the other hand, companies that are doing well and growing in product sales in these tough times, particularly in recessionproof areas, are worth considering as investment opportunities.

Back Burner Strategy. While assisting a company
with an initial public offering, I befriended a very successful underwriter. He shared with me his strategy for
success in the stock market. He selects six to eight
stocks and buys shares of these stocks every month. If a
stock price drops over a two-month period, he moves
that stock to the "back burner" and puts the money he
would have invested in that stock into the stocks that
have shown growth during the period. He watches the
action of the back-burner stocks for a few more months,
and if they continue to decline, he replaces them with
new stocks.

Get Expert Advice. If you are confused by all the investment options, you are not alone. It has become a full-
time job to track investments in these tumultuous times.
I suggest that you find a certified financial planner or
other financial professional to help you plan an investment strategy. If using a stockbroker, ask about receiving a discount or consider using a discount firm to
reduce fees.

Buy Wisely. Pick stocks in recession-resistant industries (see list in Chapter 7). Select blue chip income
stocks that have a good record of increasing dividends
over the past decade. Look at high-yielding telephone,
utility, food, waste management, health care, household
product, and greeting card stocks and companies with
little debt. Remember, companies with a lot a debt will
have to use your investment to service that debt instead
of passing it back to you as a dividend or reinvesting to
provide growth.

Bulls, Bears, and Pigs, or When to Sell Stocks. People
often have trouble selling stocks that have made a gain;
they want to wait for an even bigger gain. By waiting for
the top price, people leave themselves vulnerable. Other
sellers who are not as greedy will sell, and their sales

will bring the price down as they take their profits. When asked how he did so well in the stock market, Bernard Baruch replied, "I always sold too soon."

Don't think about the commission and tax consequences when you are going to sell; instead cut your losses quickly. Have your broker put in an automatic sell order at a predetermined price. Decide at what gain or loss you want to sell a stock. Have the broker contact you when those points are being reached so that you can review your sell decision before the transaction is made.

The past is no indication of a stock's future. Just because you had success with a particular stock, don't let a sentimental attachment or wishful thinking about past success keep you from dumping a declining stock. Unlike an aging dog, a declining stock doesn't deserve your loyalty.

Bonds

Another way corporations raise capital is through the use of bonds. When you buy a bond, you are lending an organization money and it is promising to pay back the face value of the bond, usually $1,000, at a specified time and guaranteed rate of interest. (Bond prices are not quoted in the papers on face value but on the basis of 100, so always add a zero to compute the price you actually pay.) Thereafter, bond rates rise or fall like stocks.

An advantage bonds have over stocks is that their interest rate, called the coupon rate, is guaranteed. Also, bonds take precedence over common and preferred stock in the event of liquidation owing to corporate bankruptcy, which will be on the increase throughout the 1990s. A disadvantage of bonds is that interest rates make the bond market volatile. If interest rates rise and you need to sell your bonds before their maturity date, you will face a loss because investors will prefer to purchase the newly issued bonds that pay higher interest rates.

Security is another concern when buying bonds. For some mortgage-type bonds, the security is particular assets such as planes and railway cars. Most bonds, however, are insured only by their credit rating, which is based on past and current corporate health. To determine the quality of a bond, check with Standard & Poor's or Moody's, two independent rating services. Corporate bonds typically pay higher yields than do U.S. Treasuries because they are not backed by the government.

Bonds can be "callable" or "noncallable." During a period when interest is low, a municipality or company can elect to redeem the bond prior to its maturity date. Bonds have a "call price" to compensate for lost interest if the bond is called. To complicate matters further, there are "convertible" bonds that usually carry a lower interest rate than a regular corporate bond but are convertible into common stock at a specified ratio. These bonds can appreciate in value either because interest rates drop or because the price of the stock goes up. And, of course, there are "tax-free," "partially tax free," and totally taxable bonds. The tax consequences of bonds affect the interest rates you receive.

To reduce risk in the safety part of your portfolio, buy only bonds that are A-rated by Moody's and Standard & Poor's.

When buying bonds, use a ladder strategy as described next.

INVESTMENT STRATEGIES WHEN THE INVESTMENT CLIMATE IS CHILLY

I asked experts from three investment firms to develop an investment portfolio for investing $50,000 for each of four types of investors. The investors wanted

Income with safety

Equal balance between safety and growth

Growth

Speculation for a high return (willing to risk it all)

The investment period, 1992–1996, GDP growth was projected at less than 1%, unemployment reached double-digit figures by 1994, and inflation was less than 5% over the period. Mortgage rates and long-term interest rates were 9% real interest; after adjustment for inflation, they were 5%. Business failures and layoffs continue; if a recovery occurs in 1992, it's very weak.

Strategy 1

The following strategy was developed by a major investment firm which prefers to remain anonymous:

General. Each portfolio has an equity component to counteract inflation. This is based on Ibbotson technical research which demonstrates that in every five year period of investment history common stocks have outperformed other investments.

Indeed, based on rates of return over the last 50 years, common stocks have more than doubled the return of other investments, including long-term corporate bonds and Treasury bills, according to an associate with the aforementioned firm.

Investing 100% of your portfolio in common stocks may be overly aggressive for some, but younger investors with diversified portfolios, and those with other retirement accounts like 401(k)s, can afford to be a little more aggressive with their IRA and may wish to consider investing a portion of their portfolio in equities.

Mutual funds with equivalent objectives could be used in lieu of individual securities. Those investors with larger amounts should consider individual investment advisors as well. Depending on comfort level some portion of each portfolio should be invested in cash equivalents such as money market funds.

Income with Safety. To achieve higher income, use
ladders, that is, sequential maturities of government or
corporate bonds in order to provide diversification of maturity and lessening of interest rate risk.

Investors holding short-term CDs and money market funds and facing today's low short-term rates can
improve their returns by reinvesting their money in a
"laddered" portfolio of U.S. Treasury securities, says the
firm's senior vice president and national marketing
manager for taxable fixed-income securities.

In a laddered portfolio, funds are shifted away from
short-term investments into securities with slightly
longer maturities, locking in today's higher yields.

In the 1980s, investors became conditioned by high-
yielding CDs and money market funds, and now believe
that short-term securities offer the best balance between
risk and return. This is a concept people have to avoid if
they want to capture higher yields in today's market.
The difference between short- and long-term yields now
stands at nearly 4%—the greatest in history—making
longer-term investments more attractive.

To build a ladder to fit your investment needs, review your past decisions and decide what maturities you
feel most comfortable with. Then move out the yield
curve by buying securities with slightly longer maturities than you normally would. With today's steep yield
curve, even a modest extension of maturities can have a
significant impact on returns.

A laddered portfolio of U.S. Treasury Notes may
allow the investor to improve returns by over 2.0 percent when compared to money market yield funds. (see
Table 8-1).

With a laddered portfolio, two important benefits
result. First, the portfolio immediately produces more
income due to the higher yielding investments; second,
the income is more reliable because frequent reinvest-
ment is not necessary.

The laddering concept can be easily adapted to any fixed-income security such as a government, corporate or municipal bond.

This firm believes that short-term rates will remain low. Therefore, it may be best to extend now so that reliable income can be preserved.

TABLE 8-1 U.S. Treasury Notes Laddered Portfolio

PRINCIPAL AMOUNT	COUPON	MATURITY	YIELD
$25,000	5.00%	12/31/93	5.27%
$25,000	6.00%	11/15/94	5.71%
$25,000	7.75%	3/31/96	6.56%
$25,000	7.875%	1/15/98	7.04%
$25,000	7.125%	10/15/98	7.11%
$25,000	7.75%	2/15/01	7.44%

Total Principal:	$150,000	Avg. Monthly Income:	$863.75
Approx. Investment:	$155,056	Avg. Maturity:	5 years
Annual Income:	$10,365	Avg. Yeild To Maturity:	6.52%

SOURCE: Shearson Lehman Brothers

Equal Balance Between Growth and Safety. Here, perhaps up to ½ the assets could be invested in bond ladders, as previously described. Outside a cash reserve of 10% or so, the remainder of assets might be placed in high quality growth stocks. Some global equities would also be desirable.

Growth. Outside of a cash reserve at 10–20%, this portfolio should be invested in 15–20 equities with the majority of blue chip quality. A smaller percentage should be in younger, higher-growth firms, and another portion in non-U.S. securities where that country's stock market is considered undervalued.

Speculation. For this most aggressive portfolio, a group of 8 to 12 high reward/high risk equities could be selected. Here, with low interest rates, the investor might choose to invest on margin (borrowing from the brokerage firm) to leverage the investments. This approach to investing should only be undertaken by very experienced and financially suitable investors, or through the use of portfolio advisors with proven track records.

Strategy 2

Prudential Securities' John E. Patrick,[1] like most analysts, doesn't agree with the econoquake premise: "Maybe a trembler, but eight or better on the economic Richter, I doubt. One thing the markets have shown me is that the future is hard to predict, and what usually happens is unexpected. In the [1992–1996] time frame, the projected demographics, which in my opinion will drive the economy, will not change. More people will be over 40–50 than ever before, with more economic wealth: the baby boomers will be consumers but not as in the past; instead they will be savers, investors, moving the Dow Jones and stocks to new heights; is 5000 unrealistic? Not to me.

"The United States is big and segmented; consumer purchases can be deferred but not indefinitely postponed; change of leadership in Washington and congressional fiscal integrity which would lead to a more balanced and responsible money in versus money out would instill confidence and promote a robust business environment.

"However, failure to address the environmental effects of production could mitigate some of this economic potential and move us back to the survival mentality which you portend.

"But let's assume your parameters.

Investor 1: Income / Safety

$25M in 2-year U.S. government Treasury notes

Reinvest the 2-year $25M hopefully at a higher rate; pays no risk interest income every six months.

Investor 2: Safety / Growth

$25M in U.S. government 5-year bonds

$25M in growth blue chip mutual funds (consistent average past 5-year performance greater than 25%)

Investor 3: Growth

Managed stock portfolio with proven money manager

Past 10-year track record exceeding S&P index

Investor 4: Speculation

$20M aggressive growth stock funds

$30M managed currency futures account (with a manager having proven track record 10-year average greater than 30%)

Strategy 3

Dr. Dudley Andersen, president of Thompson Andersen, Inc., personal financial advisors, presents the following hypothetical investment portfolios.[2]

Overview. "Conceptually, we can classify investment assets into five general categories: cash equivalents, U.S. fixed-income securities, U.S. equities (common stock), international securities, and real estate and other tangible assets. Obviously, there are many different variations of types of investments within (and in addition to) each of these categories, but for now consider just these categories.

"While historical data exist regarding the relative performance of each of these investment categories (as well as specific types of investments within these categories), we cannot predict, with certainty, how well each of these investments will do in the future—particularly over a relatively short term and in these turbulent times. Different types of investments perform better than others over different periods of time. As a result, a general rule of investing is to *diversify* over a group of different types of investments. Lacking specific constraints on safety, liquidity, and the like, a simple "asset allocation" model is to put an equal amount (20%) of your investable funds into each of the five categories cited. Over time, some investments will do better than others, and the relative proportion of each type of investment will change. Periodically shift some investments (buy/sell) from one category to another so as to move back closer to the original 20% allocation in each category—or adjust the allocation to that which is best for your needs and the future you forsee.

"Depending on your temperament (risk tolerance) and how strongly you feel different types of investments might perform over your particular view of the socioeconomic future, you can adjust the relative percentages of funds you place in each category. (See the following discussion, where we suggest some specific types of investments depending on investment goals.) While selection of the specific investment vehicle is important, research has shown that selection of the allocation of investments to different categories is a relatively greater determinant of overall investment performance over time. In addition, while "putting all your eggs in one basket" has the potential for the greatest reward, it also depends on which basket, and when. Research has shown that over time you have a better chance of a "good" return on your investment through diversification than without diversification—particularly if your investments are of a passive nature (i.e., when you don't manage the underlying business or activity yourself).

Portfolios for Different Investment Goals. "As noted, we can adjust the relative proportion of assets allocated to each category depending on your particular circumstances if the equal (20% each) allocation scheme does not suit your purposes. The presumption here is that you are managing your own portfolio and the investments are for the relatively long term, so the investment allocations are relatively simple and stable over time. On the other hand, if you can justify a managed portfolio by a professional investment counselor, changes to the portfolio can be discussed more frequently, and somewhat more 'sophisticated' management techniques might be applied.

Income But Safety First. "Fixed-income securities traditionally tend to dominate this goal. As a result, an allocation on the order of 20% cash equivalents and 80% U.S. fixed income securities might be appropriate. Cash would be in the form of a money market fund (with check writing privileges), possibly a tax-exempt money market fund depending on your income tax situation, or a fund invested in government-guaranteed short-term instruments for additional safety. Cash provides a liquidity cushion. Fixed-income securities would primarily be U.S. Treasury notes, or mixed maturities, or one or more Treasury security mutual funds. For higher return (with commensurately higher risk), you might substitute some high-grade corporate bonds or municipal bonds, depending on your income tax situation. Mixed maturity implies that some notes would be purchased that will mature (be redeemed) within the next two to three years, while others would have maturities of five to seven years. As the shorter-term maturities come due, 'roll' them over (plus accumulated interest) for new notes of five to seven years so that you would eventually have a portfolio with notes coming due every one to three years.

Equal Balance: Safety and Growth. "Here the allocation might be something like 20% cash, 40% U.S. fixed-income securities, and 40% high-quality common stock mutual funds. See the earlier discussion for cash and fixed-income investments. High-quality common stock mutual funds would be those invested in primarily blue chip companies that pay a reasonable dividend and/or utility companies (that traditionally pay relatively high dividends). A minor variation here might be to invest in some funds in so-called 'balanced' mutual funds that invest in a mix of fixed-income and equity (common stock) securities. Look for mutual funds with above-average performance records over the last five years.

Growth. "Here the allocation might swing to something like 5–10% cash, 10–15% fixed income securities, 20–35% U.S. common stocks, and 20–30% real estate/tangible assets. U.S. common stocks (or mutual funds) would be slanted toward smaller companies in industries with growth potential. For those with higher risk tolerances, investments might include those in venture capital funds (to the extent that minimum required investments would allow). Whereas the United States was formerly the dominant financial market of the world, these same markets are becoming a smaller part of all financial markets around the globe. As a result, global diversification should be part of your portfolio mix. The 20–30% international securities suggested here could be comprised of mutual funds investing in common stocks in other parts of the world and/or in fixed-income securities of other countries. In addition to the growth through income or capital appreciation from the underlying securities, international securities provide the additional risk/reward of currency fluctuations. Over the past several years the real estate markets have faltered, in part due to changes in tax policy. Depending on how you invest, there may be many bargains in real estate today. In any event, you now have the chance to invest in real estate on its economic merits alone, as opposed to simply tax-motivated transactions. You might consider investing in real estate through publicly traded real estate investment trusts or other real mutual funds that specialize in real estate investments.

Speculation for High Return/High Risk. "Speculation involves investing for the chance of high gain, but with recognition of the corresponding high risk of loss. A basic rule of investing is to invest in only those things where you have at least some degree of understanding of how the investment 'works.' So even where speculating, invest only in areas you generally understand (or about which you believe your trusted investment advisor understands). Otherwise, you're really just gambling. In the fixed-income area speculative investment might include those in (mutual funds investing in) "junk bonds," which provide a high yield and depending on the trend of interest rates the potential for capital appreciation (or in the other direction, default). More speculative common stock investments might include aggressive high-growth mutual funds, venture capital funds, and the like. In the international arena, investments that feature currency futures trading should be considered speculative. In the tangible asset area, funds that participate in commodities trading should be considered speculative. Investments in raw land would also fit this characteristic. To some, investments in precious metals (e.g., gold coins or bullion) are considered speculative. Another view is that such investments provide a hedge against severe economic downturns. As a result you should consider investing at least a small amount in any of the portfolios as a hedge against such scenarios. However, the larger the proportion of such investments in a portfolio, the generally more speculative it should be considered."

WHAT ABOUT REAL ESTATE?

First, accept that things are going to get worse, and second, that there are hundreds of real estate markets, each with their own dynamics, making generalization very difficult.

The days of major increases in real estate appreciation have passed. In the mid-1990s, real estate has the potential to suffer a major collapse. The real estate market is a good barometer of what's really happening in the economy. When the economy is growing, there is always a demand for real estate. As the economy continues to falter, we are beginning to see lower real estate prices. Residential prices are going to continue to fall. At the current level of income, over 60% of the American population can't afford a median-priced home.

Trading up for larger and more expensive housing will decline as salaries and wages for those lucky enough to have jobs level out and decline.

The success of investors who purchased houses in the 1970s and 1980s will not be repeated in the 1990s. Homes should be thought of as expensive consumer goods but not as investments. If you can afford a home, fine. If not, put your house on the market, price it to sell, and take a reasonable offer when it comes along. The value of your home is likely to decrease over the next five years. Therefore, a strategy of selling before the market collapses, renting for a few years, and then buying back into a deflated housing market in which builders and developers will be forced to sell at significant losses makes sense.

Consider Refinancing

Your largest fixed expense is probably your mortgage. With the low interest rates, refinancing might make sense. The rule of thumb is that to make refinancing worthwhile, rates should drop two points below what you are paying.

A loan officer with a bank in California, suggests that you consider these factors before refinancing:

1. What are total costs of refinancing? (Table 8-2 presents some typical charges.)

2. What is the dollar amount of monthly savings after refinance?

3. What length of time in months is required for the borrower to recoup total cost of refinance?

4. Does the borrower intend to be in the property long enough to realize savings? (For refinancing to make sense, the home owner should plan to keep the property for at least two years.)

5. If the borrower plans to stay in current home indefinitely, what is the current amount of principal and interest payment over remainder of number of months remaining on existing loan compared to total payback dollars on new loan?

    Other factors should also be considered:

1. Tax consequences or benefits

2. Practical reasons to pull cash out (e.g., college, debt, consolidation of outstanding loans)

3. Refinancing to a shorter-term loan to coincide with upcoming retirement date

4. Refinancing as a way to remove certain individuals' names from title or loan

TABLE 8-2 Savings and Loan Good Faith Estimate of Settlement Charges

Date   Loan#
Applicant: *JOHN DOE*   Loan Amount *$100,000.00*
Property Address

This form does not cover all items you will be required to pay in cash at settlement, for example, deposit in escrow for real estate taxes and insurance. You may wish to inquire as to the amounts of such items. You may be required to pay other additional amounts at settlement.

		GOOD FAITH ESTIMATES
801	Loan Origination Fee	—
802	Loan Discount (Points) 1.5 pts	$1,500.00
803	Appraisal (no charge at U.S. Bank)	—
804	Credit Report	45.00
805	Lenders (Construction) Inspection Fee	—
807	Assumption Fee	—
808	Document Preparation Fee	100.00
809	Application Fee	250.00
901	Interest (Short Term) 15 days.	300.00
902	Mortgage Insurance Premium	—
1101	Settlement or Closing Fee (Escrow Fee)	250.00
1105	Document Preparation	—
1106	Notary Fee	10.00
1108	Title Insurance	600.00
1201	Recording Fees	30.00
1302	Pest Inspection (Normally not involved in refinance)	—
	TOTAL	$3,085.00

*NOTE: Assumes no impound account for taxes or insurance.
PLEASE NOTE: The above Good Faith Estimate is made pursuant to the Real Estate Settlement Procedures Act (RESPA).
These figures are *estimates only* and the actual charges due at settlement may be different.

5. Many other circumstances, such as a balloon payment coming due, or a change in martial status

Abandon the House?

Some people consider letting the bank hold the bag and abandoning their mortgage when a dwelling's market value falls below the loan amount. Be aware, however, that in some states the bank can sue the owner if it loses money selling the house after foreclosure: that is, it can sue for the difference between the sale price and the higher mortgage amount. The Internal Revenue Service counts the difference as taxable income to the borrower. If you default, your credit will also suffer from this decision.

Looking to Buy a House?

With the ever-increasing number of foreclosed homes, the residential auction has become the place to shop for houses. Check local newspapers and notices posted in city government headquarters. The government has become the owner of thousands of distressed properties. It auctions them off through the Resolution Trust Corporation (RTC). Call 800-431-0600 to purchase a list of repossessed properties in your area.

What About Commercial Real Estate?

Commercial real estate prices are also going to continue to fall. The troubles of Olympia and York, the enormous real estate firm which is in severe trouble, show that the commercial real estate market has a lot more unpleasant surprises in store for us.

Investors will have to wait many years before the outlook for commercial real estate improves. Buyers will have great deals all over the country. Watch as the Japanese will be forced to sell U.S. real estate they own as the exchange rate between the yen and the dollar rises.

Look at the warehouse sector, which is doing well in certain cities. Low-income housing allows savvy investors an annual tax credit of $7,700 deducted directly from your tax bill for a $55,000 investment in a ten-year limited partnership set up for construction of low-income housing.

ALL THAT GLITTERS IS NOT GOLD

Gold, which is seen as an inflation hedge, will not do well with the low inflation rates during the early stages of the econoquake. Gold is one of the assets being sold to generate cash by rich Saudi investors as well as poor Third World women who have been forced to sell their only asset, gold jewelry, owing to the global depression.

The newly emerging Eastern European countries are also selling gold to buy Western goods. And even before this gold dumping, there existed record gold supplies produced in response to the relatively high gold prices during the 1980s. High prices generate more production, and increased production has now led to a lowering of prices. Platinum and silver will perform worse than gold since these metals are in abundant surplus and the industries that use them commercially, such as the automotive and electronic industries, are in deep trouble.

COLLECTIBLES

As the depression deepens, collectibles such as art and antiques will drop drastically in price. It will be a buyers' market as prices and actual sales will continue to shrink.

INVESTING IN SMALL BUSINESSES

Perhaps the best investment will be investing in cash-starved private ventures that are producing profits in these troubled times. Because large companies, foreign investors, and banks are in trouble, these companies have not been acquired or received the loans they need from the usual sources. Look around your area for local recessionproof businesses. Check the local classified ads for "Businesses for sale" or businesses seeking investors. Pay particular attention to solid profitable businesses in which the owner is retiring and work a payout over time. This may prove helpful to both parties. For tax reasons, the seller might prefer a steady payout rather than a lump-sum payment, and this may be easier for you than coming up with the entire purchase price.

INVESTING IN DIVESTITURE

Look for companies that are divesting divisions. Divisions of large companies will also be put on the block to improve profitability. Speak to a business broker about opportunities available in your area. Keep an ear open for businesses that are in trouble due to mismanagement but could be turned around in this competitive environment.

STOCKPILING

Stock up on items to trade and sell in the growing underground economy for use in a financial emergency.

Many of us will experience our first financial emergency during the econoquake. Stockpiling makes good sense. It can save you in an emergency. Stockpile basic items such as food, alcoholic beverages, housewares, and personal items such as paper towels, soap, toilet paper, light bulbs, batteries, drugs, candy, cigarettes, guns, clothing items, outdoor gear, shoes, jeans, socks, stockings, car parts, tires, spark plugs, garden seeds, note pads, scotch tape, seasonings, jam, soup, tea, coffee, flour, rice, razor blades, tooth paste, and cosmetics.

If you stockpile necessities, you'll have what you need to carry on even if you can no longer afford to buy these items. And you can barter your surplus for other items you need but can't pay for.

In the growing underground economy spawned by the depression, cash and barter will be the currencies that are required.

These are times for giving careful consideration to your investments and developing an investment strategy that works for you. And don't forget the importance of regular monitoring the performance of your investments: since change will be a constant during this decade, your investments are going to need to change, too.

ENDNOTES

1. Discussion is reprinted with permission.
2. Discussion is reprinted with permission.

JOBS AND EDUCATION
IN AN ECONOQUAKE

*People are the principal asset of any company,
whether it makes things to sell, sells things made by
other people, or supplies intangible services.*

J. C. Penney

If you think education is expensive, try ignorance.

Derek Bok

Never refuse a good offer.

Proverb

In this chapter, we explore the major implications of an economic depression on jobs and education. Some of the best minds in the executive search and recruitment areas share their insights into career planning in the 1990s. This chapter can serve as a handy guide to help make the important work and education decisions many of us face.

RETHINK THE INVESTMENT VALUE OF A
LIBERAL ARTS EDUCATION

Like other investments discussed in the last chapter, college—especially a liberal arts education—may not be such a
good investment in the 1990s. In the 1980s, a college education was considered essential for "success." The industries
that were hiring, like financial and business services, mostly
demanded a college education. Meanwhile, the skilled blue-
collar jobs, in which you could earn a good living with just a
high school diploma, were disappearing under the onslaught
of cheap imports and automation.

As a result, the wage gap between a college diploma
and a high school diploma widened dramatically in the
1980s. If you had a college diploma, you did well. If you only
had a high school diploma, you didn't.

Not surprisingly, more and more people are choosing to
go to college. College enrollments have been rising, even as
the number of 17-year-olds has been falling. This is because
20- and 30-year-olds have been going back to college.

But even as the number of college graduates soars, the
demand for them has stopped rising. The last two years
have seen an enormous surge in white-collar layoffs that
will not reverse itself in the next several years. Key white-
collar industries, like financial services and government, are
shrinking instead of growing. And big corporations are eliminating levels of middle management that will never return.

In all likelihood, there will be a surplus of college graduates, and that will just aggravate the econoquake. These are
the people who felt themselves secure in the last couple of recessions, so they provided a solid base of spending. This time,
the rug has been pulled out from under them.

Indeed, a report from Northwestern University, the
Lindquist–Endicott Report on job prospects for college
graduates,[1] shows that the economic slump will cause demand for graduates with master's degrees to drop 7% and
for graduates with bachelor's degrees to fall 4% in 1992.

Some 47% of the 259 U.S. companies surveyed will decrease their hiring at the bachelor's level. Although overall job opportunities for graduates with bachelor's degrees will be down a small percentage from 1991, the drop between actual hirings in 1989 and projected hiring in 1992 is 30%. At the master's level, 40% of the companies surveyed plan to hire fewer graduates than in 1991.

The people who will do well in the econoquake are people with solid and specialized technical knowledge—engineers, scientists, technicians, computer programmers, and the like. Don't be fooled by the current high unemployment among engineers—that's just a temporary side effect of the end of the Cold War as defense contractors shed much of their work force. In the 1990s, technical knowledge will be useful education to have.

COMMUNITY, JUNIOR COLLEGES, AND VOCATIONAL SCHOOLS: WISE INVESTMENT CHOICES

As you look at the growth jobs for the 1990s, note how many jobs require vocational and technology skills taught at the community and junior college level. Indeed, these schools are the best choices for providing a meal ticket for most job seekers. The costs of these schools are often subsidized by local and regional governments, which helps keep tuition and fees low. The business and government communities work closely with these schools to assure an adequate supply of well-trained employees for their organizations.

HOT CAREERS WHEN THE EMPLOYMENT CLIMATE IS COOL

The careers that will do well in the econoquake fit into three general categories:

TABLE 9-1 Employment Change in Selected Industries, 1988-2000

INDUSTRY	1988 LEVEL	ANNUAL RATE OF CHANGE, 1988-2000
Fastest Growing:		
Computer and data processing services....................	678	4.9
Outpatient facilities and health services, n.e.c...........	675	4.7
Personnel supply services..	1,369	4.1
Water and sanitation including combined services....	152	3.9
Residential care..	391	3.8
Offices of health practitioners.................................	1,850	3.5
Arrangement of passenger transportation.................	175	3.4
Research, management, consulting services	811	3.2
Individual and miscellaneous social services	571	3.2
Personal services, n.e.c.	294	3.2
Nursing and personal care facilities.........................	1,319	3.1
Credit reporting and business services, n.e.c.	776	3.1
Miscellaneous publishing...	79	3.1
Security and commodity brokers and exchanges......	449	3.0
Advertising..	237	2.8
Legal services	852	2.8
Automotive rentals, without drivers..........................	164	2.7
Accounting, auditing, and services, n.e.c.	530	2.7
Miscellaneous transportation services	141	2.7
Detective and protective services	464	2.6

(Levels in thousands)

1. Careers requiring such solid and specialized technical knowledge and skills that marketplace demand keeps job offers coming, no matter what. These careers include ones in software engineering and computer programming.

2. Careers providing services that are actually increased by an economic slowdown. Tough times for most can mean good times for bankruptcy attorneys and security guards.

3. Careers expanding so quickly in response to demographic and sociological factors that the depression has little impact on them. Regardless of the economic climate, there will be increased demand for home health aides for the aged.

The U.S. Department of Labor believes that job growth is going to be good in the following areas (see Table 9-1).

Medical Care

Health care will continue to be one of the most important industry sectors in the economy. Employment in the private health services industry rose from 1 of every 18 wage and salary jobs in 1976 to 1 of every 15 in 1988 and is projected to grow to 1 of 12 jobs by 2000.

Procedures formerly conducted on an inpatient basis in hospitals shifted to lower-cost centers such as outpatient facilities and clinics. Releasing patients earlier led to a surge in demand for nursing home and home health systems.

In employment terms, the shift is very pronounced. Jobs in hospitals rose about 10% between 1982 and 1988; in doctors offices, 36%; and a whopping 81% in outpatient facilities.

Despite the much slower rate of growth, hospitals remain the largest employer among the medical services industry. In absolute terms, more jobs will be added in the offices of health practitioners than in hospitals, despite the larger size of hospital employment.

Demand stems from several factors, some of them expected to intensify in the future: new medical technologies, a growing aged population, and the treatment of AIDS patients.

Owing to the rapid expansion of health care employment compared to other industrial sectors, seven of the ten fastest-growing occupations to the year 2000 are health related. Physical therapy, one of the ten fastest growing, is expected to increase by 57% by the year 2000. Its growth will be fueled by demographics, since 14% of the population will be over 65 by the turn of the century.

Other health-related occupations among the top ten fastest-growing are: medical assistants, home health aides, radiologic technologists and technicians, medical records technicians, medical secretaries, and surgical technologists. Also consider related fields such as medical and pharmaceutical sales.

Business Services

Business services come close to health care as a source for a large number of new jobs over the next decade. This sector will represent almost one of every six new wage and salary jobs over the next decade. Business services are broken down into the nine industries shown in (Table 9-2).

Personnel Supply Services

The largest job category and the one projected to add the most jobs over the next decade is personnel supply service, which includes the large and growing temporary help segment. Because temporary personnel help meet peak work load demands while keeping rates competitive with the cost of direct hiring, future gains are expected. However, the growth will be slower than in the past. The skill level will shift somewhat away from la-

**TABLE 9-2 Profile of business services industries
1988-2000**

INDUSTRY	EMPLOYMENT			ANNUAL RATE OF CHANGE	
	1988	2000	GAIN 1988-2000	Employment	OUTPUT
TOTAL BUSINESS SERVICES	5,570	8,311	2,741	3.4	3.5
Advertising	237	330	93	2.8	4.4
Services to dwellings	785	1,028	243	2.3	3.3
Personnel supply	1,369	2,218	849	4.1	3.6
Computer	678	1,200	522	4.9	4.3
Research, management, consulting	811	1,190	379	3.2	3.3
Detective and protective	464	632	168	2.6	2.1
Equipment rental	262	356	94	2.6	2.1
Photographic	188	241	53	2.1	3.5
Credit and all other	776	1,116	340	3.1	3.2

(Levels in thousands)

SOURCE: U.S. Department of Labor, Bureau of Labor Statistics

borers and noncomputer-related clerical jobs to computer programmers, accountants, engineers, and computer-skilled clerical workers.

Computer Services

The fastest-growing industry sector in the whole economy will be computer services. Employment in this industry sector is expected to grow almost 5% a year through this decade. Demand for operations research analysts, programmers, and related computer specialists will continue to be very high throughout the 1990s. The driving forces will be the growth of packaged software products and customized computer systems. Also, the demand for computer and data processing services will be propelled by government agencies, industry, and a growing army of self-employed individuals.

Research, Management, and Consulting

Although not expected to grow as rapidly as personnel or computer services, this sector is expected to grow a healthy 3.2% through the decade. Included in this sector are commercial, physical, and biological testing labs, market research, management services and consultants, and public relations services.

As the private sector continues having fiscal stress, the public wants more and better service. The answer will be turning public services over to the private sector. Already, private companies are running our prisons, collecting our garbage, and running our bus service. These types of services will be purchased more and more by government.

Other Business Services

The remainder of the business services industries are expected to grow at just over 3%. Included in this sector are a large variety of jobs, such as telemarketing, check validating, paralegal services, and janitorial and guard services for buildings.

Education

Public Schools. Over a million jobs will be added to education over the decade. Most new jobs will be in the public sector, reflecting enrollment increases projected for elementary and secondary schools. Employment in public education was fairly level in the late 1970s and early 1980s as the number of school-age children dipped. However, by 1983 the children of the baby boomers started kindergarten and began placing pressure on elementary school facilities. Employment reached an all-time high in 1988. As this group advances through intermediate and secondary schools, employment will rise.

Private Schools. About three-fifths of employment in private education is in colleges and universities, where factors other than population determine enrollment levels. Indeed the traditional 18- to 24-year-old college age population has been declining since 1981, but enrollment has nevertheless moved upward due to the increase in foreign, older, female, and part-time students. Future growth is expected to rise somewhat in this sector, which includes private elementary and secondary schools, vocational schools, as well as colleges and universities. Besides an increased need for teachers, there will be more demand expected for teacher aides, technicians, and administrative staff.

Retail Trade

Retail trade is second only to services among major industry job producers. Retail jobs are expected to account for almost one of every five wage and salary jobs in the economy by 2000. Eating and drinking establishments make up the largest industry within the retail division and is expected to grow between 1% and 2%, which is slower than in the past. The slow growth is attributed to market saturation and slower population growth. Retail accounts for about two-thirds of part-time workers in the economy. Part-timers are predominantly women and younger workers.

Other Service-Producing Industries

Finance, insurance, and real estate sectors are expected to add over a million jobs, with the fastest-growing industry within the financial sector being security and commodity brokers and exchanges. Other service industries expecting sizable increases include hotels, legal services, residential care, engineering and architectural services, amusement and recreation, and accounting services.

Manufacturing

As noted throughout this book, there will be few bright spots for job seekers in the manufacruring sector. Employment growth is expected in nonproduction jobs in computer equipment manufacturing, semiconductors, and related devices, especially engineers, technicians, systems analysts, and managers.

Other fast-growing manufacturing jobs will be found in manufacturing industries related to health care. Particularly strong will be optical, X-ray, and other electromedical devices and instruments as well as drugs. Although employment is fast growing in these industries, total number employed is not very large. Printing and publishing was one of the few manufacturing sectors in which employment growth has been accelerating, but future gains are expected to slow with the overall economic decline.

EFFECT OF THE ECONOQUAKE ON DEPARTMENT OF LABOR JOB PROJECTIONS

The econoquake will reduce the numbers of jobs, particularly in the manufacturing and retail service sectors. Government employment will represent a larger share of total employment. Remember, all you need is one job, so don't be discouraged if the total employment outlook is not as rosy as in past years. Go to those sectors just outlined to improve your odds in the job search.

ADVICE FROM TOP EXECUTIVE RECRUITER

Putney Westerfield was a former publisher of *Fortune* magazine prior to becoming managing director of Boyden International, a major executive recruiting firm. He has these thoughts on career planning:[2]

"1. The inexorable trends toward decentralization and delayering will continue for the balance of this century. Some may view this with horror, others with excitement. The difference lies in the frame of mind one brings to planning one's career.

"I emphasize *career planning*. That's very different from a generation ago. No longer can one look forward to a one-company career—or even two or three. No longer can one assume lifetime residence in one community. Loyalty of employee to company or company to employee has been severely curtailed. Mergers, levered buyouts (LBOs), bankruptcies, consolidations, or so-called 'restructuring' give no assurance of job stability. So one must look out for number one. Concentrate on refining skills that will be in demand in the economy of the next decade, skills that will fit the needs of growth industries.

"Success, even survival, rests on personal entrepreneurism, that is, disciplined attention to improving one's marketability.

"2. Growth companies now pop up almost anywhere in small-city America. New York is no longer the corporate mecca. Three quarters of the *Fortune* 500 companies headquartered there a generation ago are no longer there. Recently, it was referred to as "Calcutta without cows." Los Angeles chokes on almost 7 million cars for its 8.7 million people. Analyze corporate performance, and you'll find that location in a major city has no positive impact on earnings. Perhaps the greatest success story is WalMart, located in the smallest corporate town—Bentonville, Arkansas.

"Companies want to attract good people. But how, they can well ask, if those people are paying 40–50% of their income for housing. Can't we make life better for good people by decentralizing to smaller cities and towns? Can't we improve profits in the process?

"Telecommunications systems permit companies to locate units anywhere. A lean corporate headquarters may remain in the congested city, but growth lies elsewhere.

"With the concept of the large corporate headquarters fast disappearing, so are the staff jobs. Information systems are rapidly eliminating the middle-management layer. This, in turn, decentralizes and speeds up the decision-making process. Formerly large staffs processed large amounts of data. They will no longer exist.

"3. Talent will always gravitate to opportunity. We are indeed a nation of entrepreneurs. The reaction to the dislocations of the past 15 years has been dramatic. During this period the *Fortune* 1000 companies have added no new jobs to America. In fact, they eliminated 3 million jobs. But the dynamism of the economy added 36 million new jobs in that period. Some millions were service sector jobs, but primarily thousands and thousands of new companies. And most new and growing companies need a president and vice presidents for finance, manufacturing, marketing, and sales as well as well-paying, newly created jobs in all functions whether located in Eugene, Oregon; Austin, Texas; Portland, Maine; or Raleigh, North Carolina.

"4. What industries should one target?

"Information Services and the Information Providers. This industry has transformed how business is conducted and in the process has created thousands of companies. (As reported in *Businessweek*, this industry already has more jobs than the automotive industry.)

"Health care. No matter how our nation's health care costs are ultimately brought under control, all health care delivery systems need better business management, better marketing, and better information systems. And with the upcoming senior citizen bulge, many jobs will be created to care for the old and infirm, whether in institutions or homes. Look for significant entrepreneurial activity here.

"Computers and Telecommunications. No matter how strong the international competition, America will be the leader in research and innovation. Here lies continued opportunity for new company formation, for new job opportunity.

"Biotechnology. An emerging giant in which America leads the way.

"Food. People will eat. There is little chance of obsolescence or recession here. There is built-in stability coupled with new product introduction and new company formation.

"Drugs and Toiletries. For those who see the world as their career arena, America's edge in drugs and toiletries offers significant opportunity. We will continue to be the undisputed leader in pharmaceuticals, a perpetual growth industry. And everything from toothpaste to personal hygiene products will continue to find fertile markets in the developing world.

"Environment. The sins of our fathers will haunt all industrialized countries for decades. But those sins have created a growth industry and an essential job category.

"Engineering and Construction. Capitalizing on America's know-how, our companies will capture major contracts at home and abroad. It was Bechtel that was called in recently to put out the oil fires in Kuwait (for an estimated $2.6 billion). And for a decade or more at home the major task of rebuilding our infrastructure, epitomized by the $100 billion transportation bill, will ensure employment in this sector.

"The jobs will be there. Do your homework. Study the industry. Research the companies. Identify needs. Identify the match with your skills. Upgrade those skills. Find out who makes the decisions at each company. Specifically, who can hire you. And GO FOR IT!"

ADVICE FROM TOP OUTPLACEMENT PSYCHOLOGIST

Robert J. Lee is co-chairman of Lee Hecht Harrison, an outplacement firm located in New York City. Dr. Lee presents his advice about the world of work in the 1990s in letter form:[3]

"Dear Fellow Pilgrim,

Since we may never meet, I take this as my only chance to tell you a few things which could be very important as you build your career. This is my "Top Ten" list. I learned them partly from others and partly from experience. Try to remember them, and use them wisely. When you have passed the half-century mark, it'll be your turn to find phrasings for the next generation.

1. *"My Work" is more than just a job.* The most successful and happiest people are the ones who don't limit their definitions of "My Work" to their job descriptions.

    Working is extremely important. One's work is how one is productive; certain talented people even have their stuff published with a title such as "The Complete Works of . . .". One's work is a way to earn a livelihood, although sometimes this goal competes with the first one ("I never have time to do *my work* because I'm so tired when I get home from work!"). And work is an important way to be connected with others in society.

    But one's work is more than whatever your job is, at any point in time. You may lose your job or may take a job you don't want, or you may retire or be disabled or be on vacation and none of these will necessarily change your sense of "My Work."

It takes a bit of work to develop a clear sense of "My Work." Some people find it sooner, others later. Sometimes it changes. But it's worth the effort to discover how you want to be productive, contributing and connected in this world.

2. *Your life is more than your work.* A doctor once told me that he never met a dying man who wished he had spent more time at the office.

    There are many other places and ways to spend one's time and energy—certainly one alternative is with your family, the people who are closest to you. And there are many other options: extended family, friends, neighbors, the larger community, causes and people you find worthwhile, and so on. And there should be time for yourself—to digest life, to recuperate, to be creative and silly and serious and whatever else you want to be.

3. *Find your rock bottom values.* I hope that you won't have to think about this matter very often. It helps to have some conscious perspective on it, however, because "the values" thing can jump up suddenly and force you to make a choice.

    The list of possible values would include honesty, loyalty, charity, financial gain, financial security, family time, personal freedom, professional development, scope of authority, type of work, geographic location, social contribution, and so on. You can't "max out" on all of them simultaneously. From time to time have a talk with yourself, and perhaps a significant other in your life, to see where you're at.

4. Careers may not be forever. Some careers (like NFL wide receiver) tend to be very short and al-

ways leave time for other careers to follow. Some careers (like author or consultant) can be lifelong but intermittent. And others, such as musician or high school teacher, can be very short, intermittent, or prolonged, as one wishes.

But very few careers are forever. Social and technological change, good and bad luck, family developments, personal growth and health, and whatever other variables there may be in your life tend to create multiple careers for many people. When you're in the middle of one, it's perhaps hard to imagine being in a different one—but it's more than likely than not that you'll have at least two or three careers, and maybe more. Be prepared, at least psychologically.

5. *Jobs aren't forever.* Even more than careers, jobs come and go. The average tenure in most jobs is probably only a couple of years. Bosses, employers, owners, colleagues, assignments, titles, cities, offices—the dimensions of a job keep changing so much that it's not always possible really to know whether you're in the same job or a new one.

Point 1: Be aware that change is more constant than anyone really likes. There's no way to be ready to change all the time, but try to accept that it will be a regular part of your life.

Point 2: Take advantage of what you've got when you have it. Delays can be costly; windows of opportunity don't stay open for long. So ask for what you want, introduce yourself to who you want to meet, learn what interests you, and be ready to move on.

Point 3: Learn how to say goodbye so that you build bridges, without unnecessary sorrow, regret, and anger. There will be almost as many goodbyes as hellos. It's an important skill.

6. *Networks are forever.* Those goodbyes are one element in *My Network*. If you save only one possession from a fire, let it be the computer disk with the names and addresses of *My Network*. In an age of too much mobility, you will learn to appreciate the value of having people you can trust, and who share your memories. Don't lose them. Keep building your list. Keep it fresh.

7. *There are careers, jobs, licenses, and deals.* Sometimes people are working on their careers, and sometimes not. There will be times when you hold a job unrelated to any career. And sometimes you'll be given a chance to join an organization with a title but no job—this is a kind of hunting license, a chance to make yourself useful, if you can. And there are deals—risky projects with important potential. All are legitimate, but don't confuse one with the other; know what you're doing so you will have realistic expectations.

8. *Every job is political.* Too often I've heard someone say he or she doesn't like or want to be part of "the politics" of an organization. Nonsense. All jobs that involve people are political. "Politics" is the code name for interpersonal skills, as used by people who haven't learned to be good at it yet. Influence, conflict management, dealing with diversity, temporary teams, developing consensus, and participation—these are what organizations are made of, because they are made of people. Enjoy it, enjoy them, and learn to do it well.

9. *We're all self-employeed.* Regardless of your sense of contract with an employer, ultimately we're all self-employed. Folks who really are self-employed clearly are subject to measurement on the basis of value-added contributions. The rest of us are too, but it takes the system a bit longer to catch up with

us sometimes. Also, the more you provide real value for your clients, the more you'll be able to exercise the self-management that goes with real self-employment.

10. _____. The last one is for you to fill in. Try to learn from your own life experiences. Encourage others to learn from their lives, too. So, get to know yourself well enough so you can fill in this blank with a learning you find really important.

Very best wishes, Pilgrim. May your journey be both exciting and peaceful."

THE EVER-EVOLVING JOB CREATION ENGINE

Ed Winguth has operated an executive search firm, Winguth & Company, for over 20 years. He shares his concern about job creation in the 1990s:[4]

"At any given time in a nation's history, there are conflicting trends which frame one's optimism or pessimism about the future. One irreversible trend, demographics, will affect new job creation in the United States drastically and, therefore, our way of life.

For decades, the United States has been the envy of the world in its ability to create new jobs. In the 1980s, for example, while the *Fortune* 500 companies had a net loss of 3½ million jobs, the many smaller, entrepreneurial companies created 20 million new jobs. The majority of these jobs are in industries requiring education and training beyond the high school level.

"For two decades, Winguth & Company has been able to observe the founding and growth of such job creation companies from the vantage point of our executive search offices in 'Silicon Valley,' California. These have been 'high-tech,' 'low-tech,' and 'no-tech' enterprises. Our observations have been compared with those of other International Search Associates (ISA) offices around the world. Conclusion: the United States is unique in its entrepreneurial mind-set and ability to generate large numbers of new, job-creating enterprises.

"The vast majority of these businesses were founded and are managed by educated white males. But the incoming supply of these men has been dwindling steadily. By the mid-1990s, fewer than 5 percent of the individuals entering the job market will be white male college graduates. So where will the founders and managers of these job creation machines come from? Minorities? Not in anywhere near the same numbers, unless our society commits to major changes in attitudes and education. Today, Afro-Americans have the highest dropout rate. Only 3 percent of Hispanics graduate from college. Asians, of whom many achieve outstanding academic and professional success, represent only a small percentage of the U.S. population.

"What about women? Yes, they are forming companies at over twice the rate that men are. And we know from personal experience that there are many outstanding women executives of diverse ethnicity. But the pool of working women professionals and managers will continue to be smaller than that of men.

"The world-renowned U.S. job creation engine is headed for a serious decline for the rest of the century and into the next—and with it, our standard and quality of life unless we unexpectedly demonstrate the vision, will, commitment, and resources to change it."

Where to Find the Best Economic Growth?

Despite the recession, the economies of 28 states grew in 1991. The Northeast, however, which lost jobs in 1991, is expected to shrink again this year. More jobs will go throughout New England as defense spending keeps winding down, stricken banks merge and downsize, and state and local governments contract. California, with its congestion, rising crime, heavy regulation, and high land costs, has spurred an exodus to Oregon and Washington. The Great Lakes will continue to suffer with the auto industry.

The areas that have been showing economic growth include Texas and the Mountain states region.

Job Search Tips for Troubled Times

Try to Ride Out the Storm in Your Present Job. Finding a new job is going to be difficult for most people in this period of 'downsizing.' Rule 1 is: 'Don't give up the job you have until you are able to secure a new position.' Don't quit. It's much easier to find a new job while you're working.

To hold your job longer, try to make yourself valuable to your organization. Look for opportunities to broaden your skills and take on more responsibility. Making suggestions or initiating programs on how to cut expenses and increase sales or funding are always welcomed by economically troubled management.

Solidify and broaden your power base. As Robert Lee pointed out earlier, politics is a natural part of business. Business is not a democracy, and being 'right' or 'best' does not assure continued employment, but having the right connections might. Start immediately meeting people with political clout in other areas of the company. Take advantage of informal settings such as coffee, lunch, and company picnics to socialize and learn the interests and concerns of upper management.

If your department looks like the place the next layoffs are going to come, ask your contacts for suggestions about other opportunities *before* the axe falls. Accept reduced hours or reduced wages rather than be let go. Ask to stay on payroll even if your pay comes out of severance. Have a secretary pick up your messages and tell people you're out of the office. Coordinate the reason for your resignation with your supervisor and personnel. Stay with the industry associations. Ask about outplacement services offered by the company. Again, it's much easier to get a job while you're still employed, and the long lag times without a paycheck between jobs make reduced wages often a better choice than no wages.

Be a model employee. Don't highlight negatives by being absent or late without good cause. If you have been having a personality conflict with the boss, it's a good time to make peace.

Be aware and prepare for problems. Look for the warning signs of layoffs, such as continuing sales declines, hiring freeze, not being invited to meetings you normally attend, your boss being let go, your boss seeming to avoid you, your not being carboned in on memos, your performance appraisal not going well. If you see the warning signs, start right now finding another job. It's never too early to start!

Being Let Go

Work is one of the basic foundations of our life. When we are let go, we may feel shock, loss of self-esteem, embarrassment, and depression. Allow yourself some time off to feel the emotions that arise with job loss. These are healthy responses to loss, and psychologists tell us we must "feel to heal." Don't react with anger and lose your temper at your employer. You will likely need it for references, and your boss and colleagues may be sources of job leads. Do, however, play for time and use the momentary guilt of your employer to try to get better severance, benefit terms, or use of secretarial services for your job search.

Use your family and friends as an emotional support group, but, remember, the job loss is traumatic to them as well. Exercise regularly and eat healthy foods to reduce stress. Visit a therapist who can guide the family through the healing process.

Remember, you are not alone: the econoquake will affect the employment of millions of people. Accept that the effects of the econoquake are beyond your control. They are!

After you take a brief time to mourn your loss, begin your new job of finding a job. The longer you wait, the less likely you are to succeed. Don't make your time off into a vacation by sleeping in late and finding all sorts of excuses for not going about the full-time job of looking for work.

Planning is an important task. Prepare a financial review of your available resources. Take a pencil and paper and list your assets. Include your bank and money market accounts, severance pay, stocks, bonds, retirement plans, and cash surrender value of insurance policies. Make realistic conservative estimates of the market value of your home, cars, furniture. Categorize your assets into those that are readily available, such as bank deposits and money markets, and those that you wouldn't mind selling to provide a cash reserve.

Next, compile how much income you can expect each month. Include interest income, unemployment insurance, money you can borrow from family and friends. And, finally, prepare a list of your monthly expenses. These will probably include such items as rent or mortgage payment, food, telephone, insurance premiums, loan payments. Deal only with the essentials; don't include recreation and entertainment expenses.

Review these numbers and determine how long you can keep meeting payments under a worst case scenario of being out of work a year. Determine what assets you would sell and when you would make the decision to sell them. Decide how to cut expenses to reduce the monthly budget. If you decide to sell your house or find a less expensive rental, do it sooner rather than later. Stop using your credit card. The bad news about the economy isn't going to go away soon.

Your Next Job

Assess who you are, what you have done, what you like to do, and what you can do.

Taking Stock.   Most of us ended up in our present job and field almost by accident. Take time to consider what type of work will make you happy. Devoting some time to determining what suits you best and seems the wisest choice will help you avoid reacting out of panic and taking a job on the rebound. You can always ask a prospective employer for a week or ten days to consider a job offer.

Get started by asking yourself what it is that you like to do and write it down. Answer the following questions:

Do I want to stay in the same type of job or industry?

What jobs am I qualified for?

What are my short-term career goals?

What are my long-term career goals?

What did I like about my last job?

Do I prefer large or small organizations?

Once you're better acquainted with yourself in terms of employment, carefully consider your vocational, performance, and personality strengths and weaknesses. Discuss your strengths with someone who knows you—and be ready to hear of strengths you never guessed you possessed!

For example, ask yourself if you are

technical	a good speaker
professional	a good listener
specialist	a good writer
generalist	a good mechanic
blue collar	good with numbers
sales-oriented	a good teacher
artistic	a good administrator

Consider whether you are

a team player	well-organized
intellectual	a leader
physically strong	tactful
a hard worker	honest
assertive	adaptable and flexible

Decide whether you

learn quickly	prefer repetitive tasks and routine
like serving others	like details
have broad admin-istrative experience	

Don't forget to look at your weaknesses. Ask yourself if you are

lazy	loud
antisocial	slow
confrontative	sloppy

Improving Your Employment Profile. "Continually building skills gives you the flexibility you will need to move among different careers and industries. Think about adding to or improving upon your skills by moonlighting on a second job. This will build confidence and enlarge your employment network. Acquiring additional academic credentials and skills at night school is also a highly recommended way to increase your skill set.

Pick the Perfect Job. Prioritize as essential, important, and not important these parameters of your perfect job:

Safety

Security

Quantity and quality of experience to be gained

Money: how much will I earn? What do I need? What would I like?

Do I prefer a predictable paycheck each month? Or is the possibility of a big payoff more important?

Benefits: How much do I need them? What are they worth to me?

What kind of people will I be around every day?

Is what I'm doing contributing to society?

Will I feel challenged by the problems to be solved on the job?

My geographic preference?

What about commuting time and options?

Will I be helping others?

Will I work alone?

Will I work as part of a team?

Will I make decisions?

Will I work under pressure?

Will I have enough variety?

Will the work be physically challenging?

Will the job be creative?

Will the work be fast paced?

Selling Yourself When You're the Product. Before presenting yourself to prospective employers, cast a careful eye at how they're likely to see you. Then practice by putting your best self forward by selling to yourself. Prepare for this by:

Listing Your Major Accomplishments. Write out your accomplishments or achievements. Be specific: identify production time reduced, dollars saved, deadlines met or exceeded. Don't be too modest. Take credit for shared accomplishments.

And don't forget your education, including all the workshops and seminars you may have taken since graduating from high school or college. Don't ignore what may seem to you insignificant accomplishments or those achieved in prior positions; they may be precisely what a prospective employer would find useful to him or her.

To handle the mechanisms of compiling your list of accomplishments,

> Begin each achievement with an action word. For example,
>
> 'Increased sales 40% while reducing selling expense 15%' or
>
> 'Reduced costs 20% by negotiating new purchasing contract.'
>
> Prioritize achievements by the type of work that reflects your top accomplishments. This list can serve as the backbone for your resume, and you should be sure to include mentioning these achievements during interviews.

Identify Job Prospects

Now that you know precisely what you have to offer, your next step is to identify employer prospects. Identify the specific work you want to do, and target your energies to those specific areas. Identify those geographic areas where you'd like to work.

Go to your library to research all the companies that fit your needs. Ask your reference librarian for directories listing the companies, industries, professions, and locations that interest you.

Decide which organizations offer most promising prospects for the type of work you're looking for. List them and prioritize the listings. Begin by going for the top companies and the best jobs. Don't look for another troubled company which is in decline.

Strategize

Research the Company. While at the library, ask to see the annual reports of these companies. Copy the names of the key executives from these companies. Bone up on what's happening in the companies and their affiliates and subsidiaries. Have they been profitable? Are they marketing any new products? In what direction does the president see them going?

Understand How Companies Fill Openings. The ways that companies select candidates and fill vacancies varies. For example, some companies promote only from within, others run classified advertisements, while still others use an employment agency or executive recruiter, spread the word at professional meetings, let various government and community agencies know about the opening, or pursue leads or referrals made by personnel contacts.

Remember, however, that 90% of job openings are not listed. They go to people who are known quantities. Companies prefer people with whom they have personal knowledge or contact. Most jobs go to people within the company or people referred through contacts or the recommendations from recruiters or employment agencies. If you make over $70,000, you should meet members of key executive search firms before you need them.

This means that networking is what you'll need to do to establish or reaffirm the contacts to make you a known quantity. Networking is a great technique for learning about a job and perhaps even for being introduced to decision makers.

After you have identified the companies you want to work for, use your research and networking to identify a contact at those companies. Play detective; try to find a contact to invite you for a job interview. Perhaps a representative of your target company is speaking at a professional or social gathering. Attend the event and ask to visit the company. Before your visit, scope out the company by reading articles about it in the *Readers Guide to Periodical Literature* at the library. Often, company personnel are quoted, and this provides a perfect opportunity to learn their views. Pick up the phone and call to discuss the article. Send a letter to the president of the company asking for an interview. These letters are usually referred to personnel who often feel obligated to meet with you when the president can't. This approach is much better than sending an unsolicited resume to the personnel office.

Another way to identify a company contact is to find a local customer who uses the products made by your target company and ask the customer for the names of their contact.

Develop and Update Your Network. Whether you are working or looking for work, enlarge and refine your network list. First, compile a list of all your contacts by using business cards, phone lists, directories, and so on. Get out and talk to people; never underestimate the value of personal contacts. Ask people about what they do and always ask who they know; a casual connection is often enough to get your foot in the door.

Keep looking to make contacts all the time. Friends, neighbors, doctors, lawyers, tax preparers, church members, local chambers of commerce, politicians, business owners, coworkers, people you meet socially, people you've worked for. Contact everyone on the list and ask them for a couple of business contacts. You can see how this will begin to have a multiplier effect that quickly leads to many contacts.

Doing the Paperwork: Letters and Resumes

Sending out resumes is an inefficient way to find work. Mailing hundreds of resumes makes you just another faceless person buried in a stack of hundreds of resumes. Be creative and find a contact to make you a known person. If you can't find a contact, remember these guidelines when using a resume:

The resume is an aid to selecting and tracking candidates and for supplementing the interview process. Resumes are used to weed out candidates and identify potential liabilities as well as strengths. Most are skimmed for a first round of elimination and than a second or third round. Therefore, you shouldn't include information that might eliminate you from consideration. Avoid referring to age, average school grades, marital status, hobbies, and other personal items. State that references and salary history and requirements will be discussed at the interview.

Forget titles, career objectives, and your goal. Instead, show skills, accomplishments, experience, and credentials. Use the skills and achievement lists that you developed to help you write your resume.

Adopt the perspective of an employer. When employers look at a resume, they are not thinking about what they can do for you but what you can do for them. Providing you with 'a challenging opportunity' or 'an opportunity to develop your skills' is not among their major concerns. They are interested in people with proven experience, increasing efficiency, increasing sales, reducing costs, acquiring scarce skills, related industry experience, familiarity with their customer base, and increasing productivity and profits.

Summarize work experience that was more than ten years ago.

Keep the resume under two pages.

Stick to facts; be specific.

Be positive and focused, not pompous, trivial, or excessive.

Move quickly to your main points, since most resumes are just skimmed the first round.

Reread the ad to which you're responding and tailor your cover letter so that it presents you as the perfect candidate for the job.

Ask for an interview: 'I would appreciate having the opportunity to meet with you.'

Since the resume is general, try to make the letter personal: mention the mutual friend who suggested that you write or something you've read about the company.

Check carefully for typographical errors and use a high-quality paper, layout, and printing.

Interview Tips

Be prepared. Know the company you're interviewing with. Find an annual report in the library or look it up in Dun & Bradstreet or Standard & Poor's. Do a search of periodicals to be up on newsworthy events. *The Reader's Guide to Periodical Literature* is a good tool for tracking recent business events as is *The Wall Street Journal, Businessweek,* and *Fortune* magazine.

By the time you get to the interview process you must be convinced you have something to offer the company. The interview is when you let it be known what you can do. Remember, it's 'what can you do for me' that an employer wants to know.

Prepare yourself for interviewing by giving yourself mental test runs on answering the following typical interview questions:

Tell me about yourself?

What would you like to be doing in the next five years?

Why did you leave your last job?

What do you know about our company?

What are your strong and weak points?

What questions do you have for me?

What is one major problem you have overcome and how did you do it?

What accomplishment has given you the greatest satisfaction?

Keep the interview focused on what you can do for the company.

Don't apologize for your weaknesses; be open, direct, and confident. Ask a question about the company; this shows that you have done some research about it and are the kind of person who shows initiative.

Ask when a decision will be made. Thank the interviewer and tell him or her that you will call back.

Dress properly.

Don't talk too much or overpower the interviewer.

Be on time.

First impressions normally last: smile, make eye contact, be confident.

Observe your surroundings for discussion cues: What interests or hobbies might you share? Is the office one of a laid back type or would you guess overly organized? Offer compliments on awards on the interviewer's walls or shelves. Don't oversell yourself.

Remember, even if you feel desperate to get a job, any job, don't let that desperation show. Better, stop feeling desperate. If you follow all the suggestions in this chapter, I think you'll very likely land a job—and having a job is basic to survival as the econoquake rumbles through the 1990s.

Good luck!

ENDNOTES

1. "Grads Face Bleak Job Market" in *Industry Week,* Feb. 3, 1992. Vol. 241, Iss. 3, p. 62.

2. Permission received from Putney Westerfield to quote from unpublished letter to author.

3. Reprinted with permission from Robert J. Lee.

4. Reprinted with permission from Erwin ("Ed") Winguth.

REVERSING THE TIDE: POLICIES FOR REBUILDING AFTER THE ECONOQUAKE

When the people lead, leaders will follow.

Dwight Eisenhower

The greatest menace to freedom is an inert people.

Justice Brandeis

The initial task of restructuring . . . is to wake up those people who have fallen asleep . . . and to ensure that everyone feels as if he is the master of the country, of his enterprise, office or institute . . . . The high degree of social protection in our society makes some people spongers . . . . They work poorly, shirk and drink hard . . . . We are fully restoring the principle "from each according to his ability, to each according to his work."

Mikhail Gorbachev

Government isn't the solution: it's the problem.

Ronald Reagan

Leadership is action, not position.

Donald H. McGannon

Chapters 8 and 9 contained suggestions about what you and I should do to survive and prosper during the econoquake. The reasons why we have to worry about the econoquake stem in large part from the failures of big business, big government, and big labor. Yet we're still looking to these sectors for solutions. Not surprisingly, whether in our private lives or businesses, when we rely on others to solve our problems, the outcome is often not what we would have hoped. However, as individuals we may lack what we judge to be sufficient expertise to address such complex problems. To suggest some useful approaches to these problems, I will draw upon my experience, which lies in management, and that of many others, including leaders in business and government.

First, I'd like to set forth what I see as the big issues that must be faced. Then, I'd like to share my thoughts about some of the policies, actions, and perspectives that should be considered in addressing our chief problems as a nation.

Of course, there are no easy solutions to our problems. The good news is that we currently possess all the resources we need to solve all our problems, including the people and the dollars. The bad news is that the dollars are controlled by an outdated government monolith that lacks the will or a plan for making these resources available to help restructure our nation for the next century.

And the problems with the U.S. economy and society are worsening at a frantic pace. All around us, we

hear shrill voices demanding change: "House the homeless," "Throw the bums off welfare," "Decentralize government," "We need jobs," "Protect the environment."

These shrill voices deserve a response. There are
many indications that if satisfactory responses are not
given, and soon, words will be translated into actions, violent ones. The violence in Los Angeles that was sparked
by the acquittal of the police who beat black motorist
Rodney King is just a preview of future problems if deep
restructuring does not soon begin in ways that are *perceived* as meaningful.

Societal issues won't go away. We must plan for
them.

The factors discussed throughout this book that
have caused our economic stagnation will leave us with
a two-class society. As the middle class continues to decline, we are increasingly becoming a nation of ham-
burger flippers and financiers, note professors Barry
Bluestone and Bennett Harrison in *New Perspectives
Quarterly* (NPQ). America has moved from the path of
higher wages and greater equality in earnings to lower
wages and income inequality that rivals that of the
Great Depression era.[1]

As we prospered in the 1980s, we grew comfortable
and secure. But we neglected our growing societal problems. We can no longer afford to neglect the negative as-
pects of a free market economy. We will witness
increased rioting worldwide unless we come to terms
with the fact that what affects one of us affects us all.
This is true in our natural environment and in our economic environment.

The United States is experiencing increased crime,
drug use, homelessness, unemployment, and environmental degradation. As New York Governor Mario
Cuomo noted, "When the middle class and the rich finally figure out that the poor, who will be forever with
us, are the working force of the twenty-first century,

they will see that the misery of the poor is our misery. The overwhelming majority of our new work force will be Hispanics, blacks, immigrants, and women. How do we expect to compete globally with an uneducated work force barely able to keep body and soul together?"[2]

According to Governor Cuomo, President Reagan "told the middle class that they had no moral obligation to the poor, and in any case, they would be dummies to waste their money on the terminally indolent." The idea of dealing with our poor underclass is unsettling to the middle and upper classes. It creates feelings of anxiety, discomfort, and helplessness. These feelings will only intensify if we don't deal with and address the growing poverty-related problems that have been neglected in our country for at least a decade.

Given our dwindling resources, we need consensus about what the basic safety net will be for a rapidly growing poor population. How about three meals and a place to sleep, a minimal standard of health care, and basic education as a minimum. What do you think?

But even if this is all we choose to provide, doing so will be a stretch for us as a nation. If all are to be assured even a minimal standard of living, we must seek a cap on the numbers who would receive it. One way to do so is to limit immigration. Contrary to popular belief, we will have all the workers we need, and our economic ship will sink faster if we continue to take aboard more of the world's needy than we can support.

"Just saying no" to the needy will be difficult for most of us. So we should encourage and support birth control and abortion opportunities worldwide. Our dwindling resources are reaching critical levels as the worldwide population continues to increase. We must use imagination as well as technology to address the problems of overpopulation. One possibility would be to provide incentives for welfare families to have fewer rather than more children. Of course, in China, families who have more than the single child permitted to them receive not more benefits but have their benefits reduced in retaliation for failing to observe the one family/one child rule. Such a practice is punitive, punishing the child with the parents. I'd prefer to provide positive incentives for limiting family size.

WHY DON'T OUR FREE MARKET ENTREPRENEURS DEVELOP A PLAN TO ADDRESS OUR BROAD ECONOMIC AND SOCIAL CONCERNS?

Why again are we always operating in a crisis mode? Can't we foresee problems and plan for them? Our most successful businesses anticipate difficulties and devise plans for addressing them. Our least successful businesses simply put out fires—and many of them exist now as a pile of ash. Why haven't our societal and broad economic issues been given the kind of visionary thought and provided with the kinds of planning that makes for success in the business world?

Free market capitalism works. Even the former Soviets have admitted this. The resurgence of "free market" theory as the proven winner over other economic ideologies has made it the envy of most of the world. We don't want to destroy the ability or expectation of people that they reap the rewards of their work and suffer the consequences of the risks they take. We must continue to rely on the free market rather than the government to provide for us.

Although our economic system has been a good provider, it neglects policy planning. Indeed, the market economy succeeds precisely because there is no grand plan. Instead, masses of people, largely unknown to one another, make self-interested choices that turn out to coincide with the greatest good. Those millions of self-interested choices by strangers are the very engines of economic progress. Adam Smith referred to the power of the "invisible hand" where no plan is needed to cause maximum economic well-being.

"The success of capitalism," agrees Robert Heilbroner, author of *The Worldly Philosophers*,[3] and "An inquiry into the Human Prospect," in *New Prospective* magazine, "arises largely from uncoordinated efforts of individuals and firms to make money."[4]

Clearly, what is lacking in that process is coordinated long-term planning and problem solving. Each individual may have some foresight, but there is no overall foresight. The "do your own thing" nature of capitalism and our preoccupation with short-term profit has encouraged the private sector to avoid long-term considerations, not just with respect to economics but to society as a whole. Long-term societal concerns have traditionally been the domain of government and politics, not of free market entrepreneurs. But it's become all too clear that elected officials find it hard to plan past their election.

WE CAN HAVE A PLAN AND
A FREE MARKET, TOO

Conservatives, of course, could argue that if we upset the equilibrium of the free market, we will destroy our entrepreneurial based economy. But as John Kenneth Galbraith points out, "Adam Smith never envisioned a world in which the capitalist would give way to the corporate bureaucrat."[5] Many of us believe that government workers earn their living in a laid-back manner and federal bureaucrat bashing has a long history. The bureaucrat, however, is only a symbol, representing many qualities that are wrong with today's society. A bureaucrat may be depicted as a loafer, an incompetent buffoon, a good ole boy, and a tyrant. But when the captains of our large private sector organizations mismanage their private sector bureaucracies and run to the government for protective quotas, subsidies, and bailouts, they still envision themselves as free market entrepreneurs.

Indeed, our "free market" now requires tens of billions of dollars in annual income to provide protectionist support to agriculture and the steel and automobile industries. In my own state of California, prime stomping ground of the free market entrepreneur, our giant agriculture industry meets under government sponsorship to control the sale of their major produce through market boards. Also, our semiconductor manufacturers convinced the U.S. government to spend half a billion dollars for a commercial research consortium to rival their Japanese competition. And let's not forget the enormous amount of market control that rests with our largest corporations. In 1989, the thousand largest corporations conducted two-thirds of all industrial business.

To quote Professor Galbraith again, "The wholly uninhibited and self-sufficing capitalist entrepreneur and the sacrament of central planning are, each in their own way, destined for that famed dust bin of historical obsolescence."[6]

THE BIG BAD THREE: BIG BUSINESS, BIG LABOR, BIG GOVERNMENT

Business

The arthritic freaking elephants (AFEs) in big business share many of the same problems endemic to big government and labor. Mature industrial companies and vast government bureaucracies both suffer from the arthritic tendencies so common in large organizations. These stem from their being centralized and remote. As a result, many people have lost hope of ever having even the slightest impact on shaping business or society and therefore have also lost all interest in personal participation. This loss of hope of "making a difference" vanquishes all interest in personal participation.

Today's societal and economic problems are so vast that many of us feel we can have no possible control over the institutions that directly, and powerfully, affect our lives. This can lead to apathy, hopelessness—and, sometimes, violence.

Having spent decades analyzing AFEs, I'm pessimistic about seeing big changes being made in big government, big industry, or big labor.

In his book, *Time, Chance and Organizations*, Herbert Kaufman concludes that, "The survival of some organizations for a great length of time is largely a matter of luck . . . . Such longevity comes through the workings of chance."[7] Kaufman doesn't have much hope that flexibility on the part of an organization will do much good and thinks that attempts to be flexible are doomed to failure. The "ravages of time" that beset large organizations are irreversible.

"Organizations," Kaufman writes, "by and large are not capable of more than marginal changes, while the environment is so volatile that marginal changes are frequently insufficient to assure survival." Kaufman concludes that the best hope for the economy is to welcome rather than deplore "organizational replacement"—a genteel term for what economist Joseph Schumpeter calls "a perpetual gale of creative destruction."[8]

Today's econoquake is currently providing the force that will eventually lead to the extinction or at least the major downsizing of the AFEs in the business sector.

Organized Labor

Organized large labor also belongs in Galbraith's "dust bin of historical obsolescence." The antagonistic relationship between labor and management, poor productivity, and quality of union workers are major reasons for the decline of American competitiveness. With publicity about ties to organized crime, organized labor has fallen out of favor, and its membership is declining; it still, however, has significant political clout. It aligns itself in a solid block, voting for political representatives of the working class who promise to deliver on "bread and butter" issues.

Labor has little fear of deficit spending or increasing the function of government in the affairs of the country through the spending process. All labor asks of big government is that it does not interface with labor's prerogatives in the collective bargaining process. Labor will not help pressure government to balance the budget since it feels that government spending is necessary to increase the levels of consumption that raise demand and increase jobs, preferably union jobs: "We cannot afford to regard every expenditure of the federal government as a mask for big government." This quote from an old AFL-CIO economic planning policy paper still contains the values and philosophy they espouse today. Labor argues that we already have big government: after all, we are a big nation, so the issue of big government is false and deceptive.

Government

What *is* the federal government anyway? Answer: Dozens of special interest groups that share the same zip code.

If you share the widespread view that our government exists to serve the best interests of the nation as a whole, it will, of course, sound like treason to suggest dismantling the federal government. However, the public has little appreciation of the special interest groups that control our government. I'm not talking about the political action committees (PACs). I'm thinking about the federal agencies themselves, the people and institutions our tax dollars are supporting. In the legislative branch, for example, the Agriculture Department tends to represent farmers; the Department of Housing, Education and Welfare, the professionals who provide welfare and education services; the Department of the Interior, Western interests; and the Armed Services Committee, military contractors. The chief danger, according to George Shultz, who has held several top-level posts and was most recently President Reagan's secretary of state, is collusion among the various representatives of particular interest groups, the department, the legislative committee, and the organized special interest group within society.

Along with our president, the executive branch also consists of advocates of competing interests, and, according to George Shultz, policy making involves a "struggle between them." The executive office of the president has been growing in size and responsibility over the past four administrations. The executive office, through its identification with the president, who is, after all, elected by the people, should be better able to analyze policy issues in a disinterested fashion than the advocacy agencies in the legislative branch. Perhaps the independent, long-range planning function I'm proposing could be administered within the government system through the executive office.

Not surprisingly, the special interest advocacy system that has become our government and subverted our representative democracy is trying to subvert the concept of a single executive branch by all means in its power. These include the creation of so-called independent agencies that make policy without the direction or influence of the president and the subversion of the presidential budget and in its stead the submission by independent agencies of their own budgets directly to Congress.

Why Is Government So Inefficient? The very constitutional checks and laws that help preserve our liberties impede efficient operation. "Government, as we often forget, is chiefly what agencies do," Tom Peters notes in his review in *The Washingtonian* of James Q. Wilson's *Bureaucracy: What Government Agencies Do and Why They Do It.* Wilson observes that "owing to putting process over outcome, equity over efficiency, we get more or less the government we desire. "Government in the United States is not designed to be efficient or powerful, but tolerable and malleable . . . . Government can't say yes. Government is constrained. Where do the constraints come from? Us."[9] Americans, believes Wilson, "distrust anyone who wields power and sought to prevent abuse by surrounding all power wielders with constitutional checks and laws."

But, as George Shultz and Kenneth Dam point out, equity arguments are all too often used as a kind of camouflage to provide support for narrow self-interest. True, the notion of "the fair shake" holds a basic appeal to Americans today as Teddy Roosevelt's slogan of a square deal for all citizens did in his time.

Certainly, a key problem in formulating public policy is how to recognize the legitimacy of a concern for the poor and the disadvantaged but avoid having the rhetoric of poverty or minority become the servant of well-placed interests. Happily, with certain exceptions, America has not generally experienced flagrant oppression by the majority of a minority. Indeed, we are now operating from what Robert Dahl calls a system of "minorities rule" in which "public policies are the result of opinions and interests of neither a majority nor a minority, but rather [are arrived at] through compromises of various organized and vocal minorities."[10] The old squeaky wheel syndrome is the oil that moves our politicians.

At any rate, it is common to see economists and financially oriented government officials lined up behind a

relatively efficient solution and the more politically in-
clined officials supporting what they believe—or at least
what they believe Congress and the people believe—is
the equitable solution. In the opinion of R. Joseph
Monsen, Jr., and Mark W. Cannon, this system of "making public policy by minorities rule through a political
brokerage system of negotiation and compromise,
though imperfect, represents the most effective democratic system yet devised for a large bureaucratic society
comprising rival economic interests."[11]

The High Cost of Overregulation. "Detailed regulation," says James Wilson, "is rarely compatible with energy, pride, exercise of initiative." "But how can
government delegate Trust?" he wonders.[12] He concludes
that it can't. We've all heard the story of the $600 Penta-
gon ashtray. This ashtray was the consequence of adher-
ing to acquisition regulations set forth in an acquisition
rule book of several thousand pages. The pertinent rule
states that when an aircraft is turned over from active
duty to the reserves, it must come with a complete inventory even if a replacement for a missing ashtray
must be handmade to fit precisely into the allocated
spot. Following this rule cost taxpayers $600—at a time
when smoking is prohibited on all commercial aircraft!

Statutory Deadlines. The so-called "statutory dead-
line" is popularly thought of as a management tool for
curbing unnecessary delay and firmly establishing priorities for recalcitrant bureaucrats. Such deadlines require
that federal and state agencies accomplish specific actions by a certain date. But too often there is not a valid
rationale for selecting the date chosen. Members of Congress lack an incentive for assigning deadlines based on
a cost-benefit analysis, which is how a business that
hopes to stay in business sets its deadlines. Politicians
tend to set deadlines in ways that generate the greatest
amount of press coverage and constituent concern or

support—another example of planning for the short term with negative consequences for the longer term.

Expertise and the Nature of Work. People tend to do what they know how to do rather than to do the job. This seems a matter of common sense, but it has a profound influence on what actually gets done in this country. Too often, this influence is deeply damaging.

For example, diplomats, as Wilson observes, "principally deliver, respond to, and comment on written reports." The foreign service, therefore, "prizes drafting ability above all other skills."[13] One result of this expertise is that everything is heavily, though cautiously, documented.

When the Occupational Safety and Health Administration (OSHA) was formed, field inspectors found it easier "to address safety than health hazards." As Tom Peters explained, "Counting the number of missing rungs from a ladder is a lot less difficult, ambiguous, and risky than dealing with the carcinogenic potential of various substances a worker might encounter."[14]

Staffers at the Federal Trade Commission (FTC) are trained as lawyers, so they tend to seek out instances where laws are broken and emphasize the pursuit of "winnable" cases. This keeps them busy, and they feel good when they win a case, but it doesn't necessarily mean that they're tackling the really tough problems— the ones that promise no easy victories.

Agency Culture. Government agencies, like corporate America, have their own cultures. For example, the culture of the National Aeronautics and Space Administration (NASA) could be called "macho." Above all, NASA needs to see itself as strong and successful. NASA prided itself on its "we can do anything" ethos. Such excessive can-doism contributed to the Challenger disaster. It ran counter to NASA culture to admit to having difficulties.

But ignoring problems instead of solving them set the stage for tragedy.

One way to ensure success is never to risk failure. Agencies rarely take a stand that will be opposed or unpopular. Of course, given the power of inertia, change—*even positive change*—is more likely to generate opposition than a posture that doesn't rock the boat.

Agencies seem to concentrate on trying to do what they *can do* rather than what, according to their mandates, they *should do*. When agencies are driven by observing constraints instead of accomplishing tasks, it's hardly surprising that they're so ineffective.

Often, the rules that require the red tape we all hate so much were not generated by the bureaucracies themselves but have been imposed on the agencies by well-intentioned politicians hoping to ensure "procedural fairness." The *Federal Acquisition Rule Book,* which runs over 6,000 pages, contains dozens of provisions that mandate giving special attention to women, small businesses, handicapped workers, and veterans. These rules are often absurd and are a known cause of nightmares for those forced to comply.

Civil Service. Almost everyone has a favorite story or two about the legendary inefficiencies in our federal civil service. Usually, attention to nit-picking detail takes precedence over getting the job done. James Wilson recounts a vignette I'd like to share with you:

"One day in 1977," writes Wilson, a personal specialist at the United States Naval Ocean Systems Center in San Diego visited an electronics engineer working on torpedo designs. 'I'm here to classify your job,' the engineer was told, 'What do you do?' The engineer, irked by this unwelcome intrusion, muttered that he 'invented things.' The personnel specialist wrote down this fact and returned to the office. She took from the shelf the volume entitled *Position Classification Standards for*

Electronics Engineering, Series GS-855, published in 1971
by the U.S. Civil Service Commission . . . . She decided
that inventing things was not part of the job description of
a GS-15 engineer, but it might be part of an assignment of
a GS-13. She advised the engineer's supervisor that the job
should be downgraded to the lower level. The supervisor
erupted in anger. The engineer, as it turned out, was the
world's leading expert on the logic systems of torpedo guid-
ance systems."[15]

Bringing Down the Beast. How can we restructure our
large, inefficient federal government? We can see the effects of the econoquake on the shrinking of city and state
payrolls. But simply starving the federal beast won't work.
The federal government has the power to print money, and
it is controlled by special interests that will never volun-
tarily remove themselves from feeding at the trough. Indeed, instead of withering away, the U.S. government, the
world's biggest AFE, has not only survived but grown into
a mammoth of great size, however weak it may be.

There have been efforts to reform advocacy government by submerging the more explicitly representative of
the departments into ones larger and more functionally
oriented. One of these, the Departmental Reorganization
Plan of 1971 was, according to former secretary of state
George Shultz, "smothered" by a combination of the same
interest groups and legislative committees that benefit
from the advocacy system, with implicit support from some
of the representative departments themselves.

The only natural enemy of our big; advocacy type of
government, the private sector, has so far been unable to
check its growth.

What Should Be Done?

Of course, I cannot be certain whether the forces discussed in this book will actually lead to an econoquake.
Nevertheless, I am convinced that these forces are al-

ready endangering our way of life and must be dealt with. The forces shaping our economy and our lives are complex, so it's not surprising that no single "solution" can solve them. But in the final pages of this book, I want to present suggestions for some of the actions that can be taken—by government, by the private sector, by us—to ensure not only that we as individuals will survive a truly threatening economy but can as a nation embark on a course that will create a better world for us all. Taken together, these ideas comprise what I call "America 2000," for they embody my vision of what I'd like our nation to be before the close of the millennium.

Some of you will find that you don't agree with some of these suggestions. Indeed, many of you may disagree with them. Certain suggestions are likely to seem very unusual, to say the least. But if these suggestions stimulate discussion about solving our problems, one of my aims will have been achieved.

AMERICA 2000 PLANNING GUIDELINES

We must

1. Prevent the econoquake and at the same time prepare America for a period of unprecedented prosperity by taking action right now.

2. Plan for the survival of our large companies. Indeed, part of the responsibility for the problems of the auto industry was the lack of clear government plans and policies. For years, industry leaders asked government for a firm energy policy. Perhaps our current situation would be quite different if such a policy had been in place in the 1970s. The "new," slimmed-down automotive, steel, and chemical industries of the 1990s need time to make major changes and cannot be expected to make fast U-turns in response to government directives.

3. Watch our step during a period of economic transition. Our economy is in a pivotal period, changing from one that was market driven to one shaped by government spending. About one-third of our gross national product (GNP) is affected by government, whether at the federal, state, or local level, and about 16% of us are employed by the government.

4. Make jobs available to those whom the economy fails.

5. Provide for all Americans a minimum standard of living.

6. Include in our priorities repairing our environment and our nation's infrastructure.

7. Explore ways to improve our ability to compete globally.

8. Accomplish all goals without raising taxes.

9. Draw the public back in the system.

10. Switch from public to private providers of services. Work toward decentralization.

11. Recognize that the existing central government is incapable of change from within.

12. Get our own house in order before tackling the world's problems.

Policy 1: Cash Is on the Peace Dividend

An irony of the age is that by putting an end to the Cold War, former Soviet president Mikhail Gorbachev is more likely to save our economy while failing to save his own. The end of the Cold War couldn't have happened at a better time—for us! Respected military analysts argue that with the changes continuing in the Soviet Union, the $291 billion defense budget for 1990 could be cut in half by the end of the decade without endangering Western security. Of that savings, $150 billion could be freed up for nondefense purposes. Government could use some of the funds to cover the cost of converting soldiers into civilian employees through retraining and other programs. How about trimming some of our $3 trillion debt or better yet give the money back to the people in the form of tax cuts?

Besides tax cuts and retraining programs that would increase our skilled work force, two other areas would be wise investments for our future.

> *Providing indefinite extended unemployment benefits* for those who will not be able to find work owing to the employment shakeout of the econoquake is a good idea. Unfortunately, without massive government spending for jobs, the economy will continue to falter unless a major restructuring takes place. Use defense cuts rather than additional government borrowing to finance these programs. Our current policy of borrowing instead of cutting expenses is bankrupting our children's future. It must be stopped.

> *Developing an employment program* in which local and state governments as well as the private sector receive reimbursement of up to half their wage outlays for hiring people on extended unemployment is also a good ideas. Affirmative action hiring programs should be revised to include the long-term unemployed, regardless of race, color, sex, or national origin.

Policy 2: Regroup and Get Back to Basics

America needs a time-out to regroup and heal our wounds—find a basic vision of how we fix our economy, our infrastructure. Let's decide on our priorities, basic needs, and direction. We have too many problems on earth to spend billions in space and too many domestic problems to spend billions on foreign aid. We need sweeping changes in health care to provide cost relief to business and individuals. We need a major overhaul of all levels of our education system to provide the United States with the work force skills to keep us competitive. We need to fix our roads and bridges as well as our own spiritual potholes.

Policy 3: Develop a Strategic Plan for Restructuring and Downsizing the Federal Government

Our nation desperately needs better and more cost-effective basic human services. If you look at the Federal Government from the perspective of a management consultant, you will see a large and deeply troubled centralized organization that is strategically and structurally unresponsive to the needs of its shareholders—the public. Our government has grown larger in the more than 200 years of its existence, but it has not adequately evolved. Having failed to adapt, it deserves to be displaced by a more vital organism.

But it's naive to believe that bureaucrats, politicians, and lawyers would vote to eliminate their own functions. When the government does not provide solutions but is itself the problem, it's hardly reassuring to have national policies planned by elected officials and their technocrats who, regardless of their sincerity, know that reelection and funding are usually surer if they play things safe. Politicians tend to address short-term issues that demand immediate attention and to favor policies that are "politically correct" and feasible. Where do you think we got the notion of "political expediency"?

To identify the most cost-efficient systems for delivery of basic human services, I favor development of a three-part strategic plan that would involve restructuring and downsizing the federal government, making our private sector more competitive, and increasing public participation in the democratic process.

Such a plan would begin by dismantling or downsizing most federal government activities. What do we have to lose? Centralized federal government agencies are not working. Over the past decades, we have seen government grow to huge proportions and become highly centralized and remote. A major restructuring of our federal government would save billions of dollars that could be redistributed to entities that could provide services more efficiently, and the negative impacts of government interference with the private sector would also be reduced. This reduction of government interference is vital to enable the private sector to function more efficiently.

Steps to Downsizing and Decentralization.

Identify Federal Responsibilities.   First, we need to identify what products and services, if any, the federal bureaucracy should be providing in the year 2000. Are there other organizations better suited to providing these services, for example, private companies or regional, state, or city agencies? How effective is each agency's management and operations in each of the major functional areas? What improvements can be implemented and how much of a savings to taxpayers would result?

These are just some of the questions we should be asking ourselves. The "America 2000" program states that by first defining our values and goals, our policies can begin to start moving us in the right direction.

Elect Politicians Committed to the "America 2000" Program. Public sentiment should be mobilized through informing the millions of independent Americans fed up with our current state of affairs of the extraordinarily serious nature of the economic disaster ahead of us and the need for dramatic change. We should support and elect politicians who understand the seriousness of the problem and are committed to implementing the steps outlined here. We should give the project the weight and importance of the recent Desert Storm military operation against Iraq or the Manhattan Project, which, in response to the crisis of the World War II, brought together our best scientific minds to develop the atomic bomb.

Use World-Class Management Talent. This kind of talent abounds in America; we're blessed with great innovative minds. We must use them to develop a strategic plan for the United States. Top executive search firms could select a small independent team of the best management consultants and forward-thinking executives from both the public and private sectors. This group would need to be morally equivalent to the Untouchables who battled the mob and political corruption that raged in Chicago during the 1930s. The team would bring to their task fresh eyes, no preconceived views, and an "anything's possible" perspective. Government interference would be prohibited. The team would have no economists, lawyers, or politicians. It would use a "skunkworks" format that allows for circumventing the system to get things done. This approach has been very successful in the private sector.

A no-holds-barred approach to slashing through the federal bureaucracy is the dream of every consultant who has found inefficiencies in even the leanest private sector organizations. My experience suggests that old organization designs that evolved over decades duplicate functions while increasing the layers of bureaucratic control. Eliminating or reducing centralized bureaucracies will mean billions in savings, while increasing access and efficient delivery of services.

Decentralize and Privatize Government Functions and Employ Good Management Techniques. This will help bring government closer to the people and provide better services and greater scrutiny of special interests. In the real world, however, large-scale change is unlikely and, at best, slow. We must therefore use our management tool kit to upgrade and motivate today's top-level bureaucrats to work more effectively and efficiently. Introducing simple changes such as job enrichment through increasing responsibility and accountability or providing recognition for good work can actually do wonders. Try praising a bureaucrat for *doing something right* and watch the result. Since managers often fail to provide recognition for good work, enlist the aid of the computer. For a large data entry department, I recommend that an attractive symbol, such as a rose, be flashed on the screen when the machine tallies that a worker has exceeded his or her personal best in terms of quality or entries made. This system also alerts the worker's supervisor to the fact that some recognition is in order. For front-line bureaucrats, receiving more training and marketlike incentives will also bolster motivation.

Don't forget pinball psychology! Why do people stand for hours playing a pinball machine yet suffer fatigue and boredom when doing work-related tasks? Instant feedback—with bells and whistles!—is what the pinball machine provides that work does not. When we feel challenged, a game is intrinsically motivating; we enjoy what we're doing and therefore don't need a carrot or a stick to be motivated. I've recommended using the pinball principles on routine jobs such as data entry positions.

"Find Bob Gillette" is my code name for an approach for quickly learning the informal lines of communication within an organization and for identifying individuals to provide vital information or output. I asked management to provide me an organizational guide for the duration of a consulting project. A man named Bob Gillette, who was assigned to assist me on one project, exemplifies the traits to look for in a guide: he had survived many management changes, was liked and trusted by people at all levels, had solid ethics, had worked in many different areas and functions, and was not the least but interested in assuming a top-level position within management.

Vote for Mandatory Budget Cuts.   One way to increase efficiency and quicken the pace of change is to make sure your representatives vote for continued lower and lower budget ceilings, then hold politicians to these ceilings.

In the private sector, numerous companies prove that major budget cuts not only leave them leaner but more effective.

Policy 4: Reform the Legal System

We desperately need legal reform. We have too many lawyers and too much litigation. The business community is becoming scared to take the risks it needs to take for survival and feels abused by staggering legal costs, huge judgments, excessive lawyering, and costly delays. The United States has gone overboard on protecting individual liberties at the cost of endangering the future of the economy. Indeed, a *Businessweek* Harris Poll of corporate executives revealed that 83% say that their decisions are increasingly affected by the fear of lawsuits. Small wonder, with law firms grossing more than $100 billion, according to Department of Commerce estimates.

What can we do to loosen legal strangleholds? We can support efforts to limit severely the number of lawyers passing the bar exam. Let judges, not juries, set damage awards, and have strict limits on the amount of awards. We should use private arbitration and mediation services, including the use of binding arbitration, in all legal documents. Law should *not* be used for determining priorities among broad social, economic, and political interests.

Policy 5: Support Tax Reform

As George Shultz notes, "The focus of the tax structure should be revenue collection. Attempts to achieve social and microeconomic goals through the use of the tax system must be abandoned." However, I would like to see new tax incentives for creating jobs. What also would be helpful is broad reforms of the tax treatment of capital investment, including allowing business to deduct the full cost of new equipment in the first year. Business ran up large debt in the 1980s in part because tax law favors borrowing over equity financing. The government should put an end to double taxation of dividends. Keep it simple: just cut taxes for the declining middle class. As President Kennedy said in proposing a tax cut that was enacted in 1964, "The largest single barrier to full employment of our manpower and resources and to a higher rate of economic growth is the unrealistic heavy drag of federal income taxes on private purchasing power, initiative, and inventive. Our tax system still siphons out of the private economy too large a share of personal and business purchasing power and reduces the incentive for risk, investment, and effort."

Come up with billions of dollars for investment and economic growth. Raising taxes is not the way to get such sums; the way to do it is to cut, and cut deep, into defense, federal government, and space programs.

Policy 6: We Need an Industrial Policy

We need to plan for the long-term future of business to restore our global competitiveness. The econoquake will cause the government as well as many entrepreneurs who should be thinking about their long-term growth to continue to indulge in short-term quick fix approaches to business. Although our computer, biotechnology, and chemical industries are still among the best in the world, America's technology edge is being eroded as other nations invest heavily in science and engineering.

More involvement by the government bureaucracy in business policies is not what is required. We don't want the government reallocating resources from one sector to another. Nor will the naive belief that we need to support large government industry consortiums like Sematech to be the answer.

What we need is

Federal funding for state industrial extension programs such as the Michigan program outlined shortly by Tom Peters

Better information on the manufacturing, marketing, and research and development practices of foreign competitors

Identification through market research of which unique American products and services are in demand or for which a demand can be created

Our choices are to try to compete in a low-cost manufacturing economy or to develop a technology- and education-based competitive strategy. We simply cannot succeed as a low-cost producer that must compete with the likes of Mexico, South Korea, Taiwan, and dozens of other newly industrialized nations. We will continually be challenged to reduce wages and other costs to stay competitive.

We must work smarter rather than harder, emphasizing our high-technology strengths. Doing so, however, requires enormous new investments in education, science, and technology. As Peter Drucker notes, "the center of gravity has shifted to the knowledge worker. Yet no education institution tries to equip students with even the most elementary skills that would make them effective members of an organization: the ability to work with people; the ability to shape and direct one's work, contribution, and career. The 'educated person' ought to be the new archetype of post-business society.[16]

To accomplish what needs to be done, we should grant the private sector research and investment tax credits. This would be far more effective than another massive red-tape-bound infusion of federal government funding.

Policy 7: Support Regional and State Economic Recovery Groups

Regional and state economic recovery groups know their own problems better than Washington, so they're in the best position for solving them. We should achieve measurable results by developing economic recovery plans at a regional and local level. From the helicopter view of the region, one can customize job-specific economic recovery plans on a human scale rather than pontificate in the halls of Congress about using money policy to turn the economy around. These regional groups should consist of representatives of the public, private, and independent sectors.

State governments are taking the lead in attracting new business by adopting good business practices, according to Tom Peters, who shared this example:[17] "'Our customers are our reason for being' touts the logo at the bottom of a magazine advertisement. It describes how a worker went the extra mile for a valued customer, Zenith Electronics computer group. The organization so interested in service was none other than the State of Michigan Department of Commerce. . . . The states, not Washington, are where the action and innovation—is today." And according to Peters, the pitch to business is not marked by the obsequious giveaways such as the bidding for a GM Saturn site. Instead, it features a "value-added" approach that emphasizes quality of labor, capital availability, infrastructure (intellectual rather than highways), ease of doing business, and patiently attracting smaller firms rather than frantically going after the massive, but often endangered, companies.

Michigan's story, according to Peters, reaches beyond the Department of Commerce. The state freed a portion of the state pension fund from conservative investment regulation to create a multimillion-dollar venture capital fund, one of the largest public sector venture capital pots available in the United States. This clearly signaled Michigan's determination not to leave all its eggs in the basket of the Big Three automakers. Other programs include a fund that supports bankers with insurance to backstop riskier than normal loans to innovate business; innovative retraining programs; and top-level conferences to spur partnership among business, labor, and government.

The Michigan Modernization Service (MMS) "agents" are not state employees—who would not be credible as industrial consultants—but private sector experts who would help midsized businesses adopt new manufacturing technologies. The Michigan Business Ombudsman (MBO) continually cuts through red tape to get outdated laws thrown off the books. "Most [state employees]," according to Dick Allen, MBO's director, "respond to problems with the idea killers, 'We can't do it.' 'It's against the law.' But even if it is, I gently remind them that the U.S. Constitution only restricts the people of Michigan from making war and interfering with interstate commerce."[18] Allen concludes that the "important point is to get my associates to take individual responsibility and move to an emphasis on results rather than the usual state employee's emphasis on process." Peters reports that Allen's approach seems to be working, spearheaded by a commitment to a 72-hour maximum to reply to any query.

The Future Rests With Our Smaller Market-Oriented Firms. Among my heros are the real market-oriented entrepreneurial firms, small and medium-sized businesses. These innovative firms do operate under

classic free market rules. These firms need services—
real services, not lip service, which seems to be the only
product of the federal bureaucracy.

In the past five years, U.S. overseas trade has contributed about 30% of our real economic growth. The
United States should help U.S. companies gain access to
foreign markets. The problems of small and medium companies that are trying to compete are illustrated by Gene
Biggi, president of Beaverton Foods. He shares some of the
problems he encountered in the last several years shipping
to six foreign countries.

"Before I shipped to these countries, I went to trade
shows through the U.S. Department of Agriculture, purchased booths and surveyed the competition. In all the
countries we went to—many customers were desirous of
companies that manufactured American products. We
were unique and had items not available in these foreign
countries. "However, here are the problems that faced all
food manufacturers in the United States. Foreigners could
ship specialty items into the United States with much less
regulation and duty, sometimes ranging as much as 30%
difference. It's much higher in cost for the U.S. manufacturers to ship the same product to these foreign countries.

"We are required to hand-tag each individual jar
when we ship export to all foreign countries, stating
name of distributor. The United States does not require
this when importing. This is a tremendous savings to the
importer.

"There are many ingredients we cannot ship. These
same foreign companies use the same ingredients; however, we can't ship them. The United States does not require the same conditions and yet the government says
we have an open market.

"In addition, all ingredients are analyzed and they
always seem to find something to reject. This is risky
and very expensive for U.S. companies. Foreigners are
not faced with these problems in the United States.

"I have personally boycotted all trade shows until doing business with foreign markets is on an even playing field . . . . The above conditions are the reason the U.S. manufacturers are not doing more exporting."

Policy 8: Bringing Back the Public

A decade or two ago, my former SRI colleagues Hewitt D. Crane and Doug Englebart were actively searching for tools to help increase public participation to solve significant social problems such as those we are facing today. Crane and Englebart were among the early pioneers who helped develop the "power tools and systems for knowledge workers" that evolved into the information systems that today we take for granted. These include, of course, the computer.

In his book *The New Social Marketplace—Notes on Effecting Social Change in America's Third Century,*[19] Crane looks back in our history at the systems and the structures that increased public involvement in making the decisions that shaped their lives then. He sought to find an analog that could be used today.

> Early American society was composed mainly of individuals and their small associations: the private sector was a highly decentralized system of small-scale entrepreneurs, and the national government was an almost invisible force in daily life. Modern America, standing now on a vast base of semi-autonomous corporations and a very large government, is a much different society. Many people maintain that our current problems can be solved by greater consciousness and social responsibility within the private sector and by a committed, resourceful, streamlined government sector. Even if this was possible, it would not alter the nature of the interactions of the major systems within society.[20]

THE NEW INDEPENDENTS

According to Alexis de Toqueville, the Frenchman whose writings in the early 1800s remain without peer for their perceptive insights about the American people, there is a "characteristically American tendency" to form groups and myriad civil associations and that these convey such an enormous power to the people that they can counteract the overwhelming power of government.

Crane believes that one key to a new structural evolution is the reintegration of voluntary/not-for-profit organizations, what R. C. Cornuelle in *Reclaiming the American Dream* calls the "independent sector" of society.[21] In the nation's early years, Cornuelle notes, this sector took on a major burden of individual and local problems, from the care of the sick and underprivileged to education. However, with the growth of population, advancing technology, massive industrialization, and the increasing scale of both public and private organizations, the independent sector has grown weak and disorganized. Although its dimensions are fantastic and its raw strength awesome, it has been performing badly. Like the public and private sectors, the independent sector would not be capable of planning and implementing the massive restructuring of government and big industry that I believe is essential for our prosperity in the next century.

Although the independent sector has its limitations, it can provide a major contribution toward restructuring. It does open new channels of communication and is a positive force to help move the nation in new directions.

To break the hold of big government, the independent sector could be expanded to include all those interested in reforming and bringing the government back to honor the principles upon which this nation was founded. It would include those who understand that our current two-party system can't and won't reform itself but who don't want to join the extremist fringes of the political spectrum. Such an independent sector could provide planners with the public mandate required for modernizing, downsizing, and restructuring our outdated central government and developing new approaches to solving our economic and social ills.

First, the newly expanded independent sector must elect people who can provide a mandate for developing "America 2000" and will provide support to make it stick.

Second, the independent sector can perform the important task of monitoring its constituents' values and issues; it can tell planners what constituents think about the process and what should and should not be included in the plan.

THE SOCIAL MARKETPLACE

How these social ideas can be effectively developed, negotiated, and communicated is something to which Crane has given considerable thought. Like physical goods such as neckties and shoes that are traded in our free market, Crane tells us that social goods (ideas) are shaped by their proponents and must eventually be sold and bought in the world of social commerce, where voters and legislators examine the goods and select among them. For social policy to be reasonably founded, the public must have a clear idea of the trade-offs between competing ideas and limited resources.

To provide the public with a clear understanding of the options, we must extend the marketplace for knowledge and information.

Until recently, Crane explains, our social planning model was similar to the professional/client relationship. The "pros," our representatives of government and large business, were the presumed keepers of competence who "knew best." We, the public, were the clients who lived with decisions made for us by the pros. I agree with Crane that now the public wants to be more involved in making the decisions they must live by. In fact, the public is becoming the third leg of a triangle that includes the government and business sectors.

However, as a public we lack the kind of expertise
most of us bring to buying shoes or neckties. Nor is there
a *Consumer's Report* we can consult to let us "bone up"
before we're forced to buy or reject an idea that is bound
to impact us, for better or for worse, far more than any
necktie ever could! Unlike the commodities markets that
have brokers and a highly developed distribution system, individuals have few vehicles for learning about
and distributing their ideas.

Crane has some innovative suggestions for remedying
this situation. They include establishing media knowledge
centers, regional exploration-brokerage centers, and—my
favorite—using modern traveling shows modeled after the
old-time Chautauqua shows that crisscrossed the country
at the turn of the century, bringing culture, knowledge,
and entertainment to small towns linked only by dirt
roads and train tracks. Of the Chautauqua, Joseph Gould
in *The Chautauqua Movement* notes:

> "It was praised for having done more toward keeping American
> public opinion informed and alert and unbiased than any other
> movement . . . . Traveling Chautaqua brought to the attention
> of millions of Americans an impressive number of new ideas
> and concepts, many of which might never have received the
> popular support that guaranteed their acceptance. The gradua-
> ted income tax, slum clearance, juvenile courts, pure food laws,
> the school lunch program, free textbooks, a balanced diet, phys-
> ical fitness, the Camp Fire girls, and the Boy Scout move-
> ment—all these and many more were concepts introduced by
> circuit Chautauqua."[22]

To educate today's public, Crane proposes modern
traveling shows that would facilitate face-to-face interaction between various specialists and leaders, planners,
individuals, and communities. He envisions a broad base
of interactive exhibits, booths, video theater, mobile
bookstores, talks, and debates. In this age when watching television has replaced interacting with real people, I
think that Crane's idea has great merit and deserves to
be tried. On TV, it's all too easy to dismiss poverty,

crime, murder, and violence; if a commercial doesn't temporarily intervene, you can always switch the channel. Hearing *real people tell it how it really is* and suggest how much better our lives could be would be a novelty. I think people would listen.

I wrote this book to bring my ideas into the social marketplace. I'm looking for buyers or people who want to trade their ideas about policies that will shape America.

I'm a realist, however, and am pessimistic about the public's willingness to tackle the major problems. People do not care what's happening in politics, nor do they know much about political events or share in making decisions. Americans have always been lethargic voters, and this has allowed special interest groups to define and legislate in the "public interest." But as Robert Dahl in *The Makings of Public Policy* points out, "An individual is unlikely to get involved in politics unless he believes the outcome will be relatively unsatisfactory without his involvement. The percentage of voters rises sharply in depression years."[23]

Wouldn't it be ironic if the legacy of the econoquake were to bring our country a period of great prosperity as well as greater participation in the democratic process? Cheers!

ENDNOTES

1. From "The Spoils of Victory" by Mario Cuomo, Ralph Nader, Barry Buestone and Bennett Harrison in New Perspectives Quarterly, Fall, 1989, p. 26.

2. Ibid.

3. Robert Heilbroner, *The Worldly Philosophers*. Simon & Schuster, New York, 1986.

4. From "The Triumph of Capitalism" by Robert Heilbroner, Joseph Schumpeter, Michael Milden,

and Peter Drucker in *New Perspectives Quarterly,* Fall, 1989.

5. Galbraith and Fukuyama, op. cit., p. 46.

6. Galbraith quote, ibid.

7. From a book reviw in *The Washingtonian* by Tom Peters entitled "Damn Bureaucrats"; Nov. 1989.

8. Joseph Schumpeter quote is taken from the same Tom Peters book review, quoted by permission.

9. James Q. Wilson. *Bureaucracy: What Government Agencies Do and Why They Do It.* Basic Books, New York, 1989.

10. *The Makers of Public Policy,* by R. Joseph Monsen and Mark W. Cannon, McGraw-Hill, San Francisco, 1965, p. 76.

11. Monsen and Cannon, op. cit., p. 324.

12. From Tom Peter's review of this book *Bureaucracy: What Government Agencies Do and Why They Do It.*

13. Ibid.

14. Ibid.

15. Ibid.

16. From *The Post-Business Society* in *New Perspectives Quarterly,* Fall, 1989, p. 23.

17. From Tom Peter's syndicated newspaper column, TPG Communications, all rights reserved. Reprinted with permission.

18. Ibid.

19. Hewitt D. Crane, *The New Social Marketplace— Notes of Effecting Social Change In America's Third Century.* Ablex Publishing Corporation, Norwod, New Jersey, 1980, pp. 23-27.

20. Ibid.

21. Ibid.

22. Crane, op. cit. p. 55.

23. Monsen and Cannon, op. cit., p. 320.

APPENDIX

SOME THOUGHTS TO CONSIDER WHEN APPLYING CREATIVITY TECHNIQUES IN INDUSTRY[1]

Our experience utilizing creative problem-solving and idea-generating methods both internally at the Stanford Research Institute (SRI), and externally at companies in a variety of industries, has led to the evolution of certain points that we feel are important to successful application. Each point is simple by itself, but collectively they all play a part in creating, what we term a "creative climate." For example;

- We have found that advanced preparation for creativity sessions is desirable. Learning and thinking about the product / service ahead of time or reading relevant articles and studies prepares a participants' mental state of mind before engaging "in a search." Walking into a creativity session "cold" and automatically expecting a flow of good ideas is designed for disappointment. Much of the criticism against brain-storming stems from this latter expectation.

- We feel that creativity should be expected from every area of the organization. Granted that the impact of ideas will vary according to one's expertise and domain or area of concern; however, the company should expect all personnel to "create" and not limit its expectations to the scientists in R&D. Consequently, our approach is not to limit a "search group" to "the scientists" or personnel from any one area—even if they are the most knowledgeable group or most concerned about the topic at hand. We feel that others can act as "catalysts," as the next point discusses.

- People with backgrounds far removed from the product/service at hand are good stimulators in problem-solving groups. For example, we observed that a group of metallurgists convened to find new uses for a particular metal focused inordinately on the liabilities of the metal. The fruitful ideas came from people outside the metallurgical domain who were not versed on the metal's characteristics at all (e.g., from biomechanics, lasers, robotry, optics—people who were pushing the "state of the art" in other areas). We have observed the same phenomena when other teams were limited to the "experts most closely associated with the search." Our approach, then, is to staff search groups with a few experts to provide a data base of information but also to add what we term "wild cards" or people outside of the topical area as well.

- We have found that it is somewhat inhibiting for a group to contain guests or onlookers who are there to "view the proceedings." First, the intelligence of the guests should be utilized—regardless of whether they are "experts" (see previous point)—but moreover, they are invariably perceived as judges. Involve them fully as members of the team or not at all.

- We have demonstrated (to ourselves at least) that creative problem-solving techniques are subsidiary to the caliber of people who are addressing the problem. Participants' attitudes, willingness to experiment, educational and work backgrounds, and even a willingness to "play games" are more relevant to success than are the techniques. People who have broad backgrounds and are familiar with more than one field of specialty should be sought out for idea sessions.

- We feel that it is important to establish a "creative climate" for a group conducting a search, that is, by establishing an appropriate physical climate through use of a relaxed setting, visual aids, availability of coffee and refreshments; by encouraging informal dress, and so on; by establishing an appropriate psychological climate by avoiding use of "idea killers", and by deferring judgment on the ideas initially generated. Since, however, there seems to be a need to judge ideas eventually, announce to the group that the ideas will be screened or sorted during a "judgment day" or session. Knowing that such a session is planned seems to keep the idea-generating sessions relatively free from negative statements.

- Another point has to do with the propriety or identity of the ideas that are generated during the sessions. We have found that some of the best ideas (as noted by group members during the idea judgment sessions) were contributed by many, rather than by one member of the group—emerging bit by bit in building-block fashion. To encourage contributions by many members we have avoided labeling or tying an idea to one person as it emerges. Our approach simply is to publicly record all ideas that emerge on flip charts entitled "Group Memory" for all to see (and to relieve the "thinkers" from the task of keeping notes or taking time to keep track of the ideas), but references to specific ideas and people are omitted unless the recorder wishes to ask for further details later (i.e., does not wish to stall a group that has generated momentum).

- We have found that it is important to focus on the substance of the problem (what, we term, "focus of the search") rather than problem-solving procedures per se. For example, we find that it is distracting to say, "We will move through the nine steps of . . . ," and so forth. We find that many of the creative problem-solving techniques have a "triggering mechanism" or step that often is the point of departure for generating thoughts or ideas. Thus, we place emphasis on the problem or focus of the search and the technique's "triggering mechanism," that is, going directly from an analogy, association, or matrix to the idea rather than compulsively working through steps 1, 2, 3, and so forth.

- We feel that it is necessary to employ a variety of techniques if the sessions will last beyond a few hours. This should also include other means to "keep the group" productive and interested, such as alternating between large groups/subgroups/individual thinking sessions and giving members the means to express themselves in a variety of ways (blackboards, flip charts, personal notes, besides the usual verbal responses). We use a large room that can accommodate "papered walls," many flip charts and lends itself to "workroom rather than a passive conference atmosphere." Besides keeping the group interested and motivated, these points help ensure that ideas will be expressed by all members of the group and not just from a few dominant and/or articulate individuals.

- We feel that it is preferable to apply techniques subtly. That is, it is somewhat inhibiting to say, "Let's sit and create," or "We are now going to use the . . . technique to think of a new idea." A group searching for new ideas does not have to be versed in a particular technique nor even know its name to be able to use it as a stimulus. One can merely state that "the following matrix will be used as a point of departure" rather than, "We are now going to employ the Morphological Analysis Approach to . . . ."

- People tire quickly when engaged in "free-floating" or unstructured brain-storming sessions. When this happens, we have observed that they can still work and generate ideas if their thinking is channeled down new paths via, for example, direct associations, analogies, matrices, product samples, even articles or advertisements, as well as other specific or more structured exercises.

- We find that it is good to have a schedule or agenda for any session lasting more than a day. This helps channel the group in a particular direction or toward some goal rather than allowing them to "float." However, the schedule should not be rigidly followed if ideas are emerging—one of the best announcements to make is that the group is "behind schedule because they have been generating results."

- Typically, we find that three to five days is ideal for "search sessions." The time depends upon the magnitude of the problem or "focus," but anything more we find is tiresome and anything less is somehow viewed as "not important enough to be adequately prepared." Give a half or whole day off to "incubate" or think privately on the fourth day of a five-day session—because we find that participants are tired by this time (even of each other). However, we feel that it is important to give participants some general guidelines for the individual thinking sessions rather than leaving it totally unstructured. Our best results have come when we have provided general examples or even Delphi studies of the future (that relate to the focus of the search) rather than to expect participants to think privately on their own during the "incubation period" (though many do not need any stimulation).

- We find that the last day or half day is fine for judging the myriad ideas that have emerged during the week. Doing this earlier would be premature—not doing it misses some important concerns about the feasibility of certain ideas that could have dire consequences later, if not addressed early.

- We feel, though, that those who conduct the sessions should assume a catalytic or "low-key" role because they can inhibit or even antagonize a group by acting as lecturers, judges, or even "session leaders." Our best results have occurred when members of a group felt that the "leaders" did not have to push, or did not get a chance to use all of the techniques they were prepared to use and, as a result, appeared to be somewhat "passive." We take the latter as a compliment.

- We feel that it is important to involve managers and decision makers in "new idea sessions" to increase the chances of implementation after ideas have been generated. Limiting involvement solely to those who may not be in a position of authority often results in more ideas that must "be sold to management." On the other hand, a spontaneously generated idea from a group that involves managers, marketing, *and* technical people has automatically received its initial market, economic, and technical screening and has a "running start" towards implementation in that organization.

- We have found that many ideas emerge from humorous and even "bizarre" statements (and probably from the release of tension associated with laughter) so . . . use humor . . . use humor . . . use humor whenever possible.

These generalizations are simply based on personal observations and usage. Although they are not supported by quantitative data, we feel they are precepts to consider for successfully applying idea-generating and creative problem-solving techniques.

ENDNOTES

1. Reprinted with permission from Joe Grippo.

INDEX

A

AAA-rated insurance
  companies, buying bonds
  insured by, 48
Accounts payable, taking
  discounts on, 134
Accounts receivable,
  aggressive action toward,
  133-34
Acer Group, 24, 25
Acquisitions, *See* Mergers and
  acquisitions
ADM (Archer Daniels
  Midland Company), 129-30
Advertising industry, reduced
  client spending and, 21-22
AFE theory, 114-16, 118, 119,
  217-18, 225
Age discrimination, 111-12
Agency culture, government,
  223-24
Agenda, creativity sessions,
  251
Age of Unreason, The (Handy),
  121
Airline industry, 11

Allied-Signal Corporation, 26
America 2000 planning
  guidelines, 226-39
  cash in on peace dividend,
    227-28
  industrial policy, 234-36
  legal reform, 233-34
  public participation, 239
  regional/state economic
    recovery groups, 236-39
  regroup, 228-29
  restructure and downsize
    government, 229-33
  tax reform, 234-36
Andersen, Dr. Dudley, 167-72
Apple Computer, 9, 72
Arthur Young & Company, 73
Assets, liquidating, 148-40
Asset values, collapse of, 43-44
Automobile industry, 6-8, 19,
  25, 57-68, 131
  AFE management in, 118
  changing marketplace of,
    7-8
  customers, 61
  gas crunch and, 58
  great mistakes of, 57-67

layoffs in, 19, 61

B

Baby-boomers:
    end of optimism of, 104-5
    retirement of, 107-8
    social security benefits
        and, 107
Baby bust generation, 99-101
Back burner strategy, 160
Bank failures, 8, 15, 69
Banking and financial service
    sectors, unemployment in,
    21
Bank money market accounts,
    157
Bank of America, 4
    Security Pacific merger, 26,
        69-70
Bank of Japan, 71
Bankruptcies, 9, 15, 35, 41,
    44, 53, 188
Banks:
    consolidations of, 69-70
    real estate defaults and, 43
    selecting, 153-54
Bank savings account, 156-57
Barger, Harold, 81
Beaverton Foods, 127-29
Biggi, Gene, 127-29, 238-39
Biotechnology, 73, 131
    job opportunities in, 190
Bluestone, Barry, 213
Bonds, 47-49, 161-62
    compared to stocks, 161
    security for, 162
Borrowing, 2-3, 152
Budget, living within, 150
Burns, Arthur F., 80-81, 82
Business:
    AFEs in, 217-18
    buying opportunities, 136
    cutting expenses, 132-33
    diversifying/selling, 131
    government regulations,
        143-44

international
    marketplace,
    growth of, 144-45
Japanese investment
    activity, 144
niche markets, 128-29, 132,
    144
protectionism, 144
redefining, 130-31
starting your own, 136-37
strategic marketing plan,
    developing, 137
strengths/weaknesses,
    developing list of, 142
Business and growth
    opportunities, 113-46
Business cycles, 14-15, 79-84
    contraction phase, 14-15
    expansion phase, 14
    recycling, 79
Business incubators, 124-25
Business management styles,
    114-16
Business sectors,
    stagnation/consolidation of,
    6-11
Business services, job
    opportunities in, 184,
    185-86

C

Callable bonds, 162
Cannon, Mark W., 222
Career choices, 181-87
    business services, 184,
        185-86
    computer services, 185
    consulting, 185
    education, 186
        executive recruiter,
            advice from, 188-91
    finance/insurance/real
        estate sectors, 187
    management, 185
    manufacturing, 187
    medical care, 183

outplacement psychologist,
  advice from, 192-96
personnel supply services,
  184-85
research, 185
retail trade, 186-87
Career planning, importance
  of, 188
Cavanagh, Dick, 121
Certificates of deposit (CDs),
  155, 164
Chautauqua Movement
  (Gould), 242
Checking accounts, 157
Chilly investment climate:
  hot careers in, 181-87
  investments in, 162-72
Chrysler Corporation, 19, 25,
  131
  See also Automobile
    industry
Citibank, 132
Cities:
  decline of, 104
  economies of, 28
Civil service, 224-25
Clothing costs, 42
Cognetics, Inc., 71
Collectibles, 176
Colmen, Ken, 119-20
Commercial rentals,
  consolidating, 135-36
Common stocks, 157-58
Community college education,
  181
Computer industry, 8-9, 13,
  42, 72-73
  job opportunities in, 190
Computer services, job
  opportunities in, 185
Consolidations, 9-11, 74, 188
Construction, job
  opportunities in, 191
Consulting, job opportunities
  in, 185
Consumer confidence, 39,
  52-53
Consumer Report's Buying
  Guide, 6-7

Contraction phase, business
  cycle, 14-5
Cornuelle, R. C., 240
Corporations, decentralization
  in, 188-89
Cost-cutting techniques,
  132-36, 152-53
Council on Competitiveness, 9
Crane, Hewitt, 88, 239, 241-43
Creativity sessions:
  attendees, caliber of, 248-49
  channeling thinking down
    new paths, 251
  creativity climate,
    establishing, 249
  experts at, 248
  focus of the search, 249-50
  "Group Memory" flip
    charts, 249
  guests/onlookers at, 248
  humor, use of, 252
  interest-holding
    techniques, 250
  judging ideas, 252
  leaders, 252
  length of, 251
  managers/decision makers'
    involvement, 252
  personnel and, 247-48
  preparing for, 247
  schedule/agenda, 251
  subtle application of
    techniques, 250-51
Creativity techniques,
  applying, 124-26, 247-53
Credit card balances, paying
  off, 152
Crow, Trammell, 70
Cuomo, Mario, 213-14
Customers:
  buying behavior of, 142
  observing, 141

D

Dahl, Robert, 221, 243
Dam, Kenneth, 221
Debt:

reducing, 151-53
refinancing, 135
Decentralization, 188-89
Defense budget, cutting, 228
Defined benefit plans (DBP),
50
Defined contribution plans
(DCP), 50
Demographic trends:
identifying, 140
impact on markets, 140-41
Departmental Reorganization
Plan of 1971, 225
Department of Labor job
projections, effect of
econoquake on, 188
Depression, 28-31, 98-99
best case scenario, 29
definition of, 37-38
most likely case scenario,
30-31
worst case scenario, 29-30
Digital Equipment Corp.
(DEC), 26, 72
Diversification, 131, 132, 168
Divestitures, investing in, 177
Dow Jones Industrial
Average, 44-45
Drucker, Peter, 235-36
Drugs/toiletries, job
opportunities in, 190-91
Dworkin, Earl, 134
Dying, 112

E

Early warning signs,
breakdown of, 13-15
Earthquake metaphor, 1-15
Econo 2000 planning model,
137-43
customers, observing, 141
demographic trends:
identifying, 140
impact on markets,
140-41
economic scenario,
highlighting, 137-38

marketing niche,
examining, 139-40
Econo 2000 system, 92-95
Economic growth, where to
find, 197-98
Economic Strategy Institute,
4-6
Econoquake:
effect on Department of
Labor job
projections, 188
effect on society, 97-112
investing during, 147-78
jobs and education in,
179-210
rebuilding after, 211-45
strategies for prospering
during, 130-32
Econoquake managers:
Biggi, Gene, 127-29
Painter, Jack, 129-30
Rosen, Jim, 126-27
Econoquake slippery slope
theory, 159
Education:
community and junior
colleges, 181
job opportunities in, 186
liberal arts education,
rethinking, 180-81
overhauling system, 229
vocational schools, 181
Elderly, 49-52, 108-12
social security benefits
and, 109
Electronics industry, 6
Employment profile,
improving, 202-3
Energy costs, 42
Engelbart, Doug, 88, 239
Engineering, job opportunities
in, 191
Environment-related
industry, job opportunities
in, 191
Equal Employment
Opportunity Commission
(EEOC), age discrimination
suits and, 112

European downturn, 26
Executive Life, collapse of,
    49-51
Executive recruiter, advice
    from, 188-91
Expansion phase, business
    cycle, 14
Exports/export markets,
    73-75, 132

F

Fantastic Foods, 126-27
FEB group, *See* Forward-end-
    of-the-business (FEB) group
Federal Acquisition Rule
    Book, 224
Federal Deposit Insurance
    Corporation (FDIC), 30, 69,
    153, 156
Federal government, *See*
    Government Federal
    Housing Authority (FHA),
    31
Federal Reserve, 29, 30-31,
    39, 48, 77
Finance sector, job
    opportunities in, 187
Financial collapse, 37-38
Financial markets, 38-39
First Capital, collapse of, 50
Fixed expenses, debt
    reduction and, 151
Food costs, 42
Food industry, job
    opportunities in, 190
Forces shaping the future,
    97-112
    age discrimination, 111-12
    baby-boomers:
        end of optimism of, 104-5
        retirement of, 107-8
    baby bust generation,
        99-101
    cities, 104
    dying, 112
    global economic depression,
        98-99

immigrants, 103
minorities, 101-3
older Americans, 108-12
politics, 108
women, 104
yuppie shock, 105-6
Ford Motor Company, 4, 25
Forecasting technique, 92-95
Forecasts, 77-95
    recycling business cycles, 79
    straight-line projections, 78
Foreign aid, cutting, 229
Foreign-owned debt, 2-3
Forward-end-of-the-business
    (FEB) group, installing,
    119-20
Forward thinkers, on board of
    directors, 120-21
401(k) plans, 50-51
Free market capitalism,
    215-17
Futurists, econoquake and, 86

G

Galbraith, John Kenneth, 216,
    217, 218
General Electric, 6, 19, 132
General Motors, 6-8, 25, 26,
    114, 132
    See also Automobile
        industry
Ginnie Mae, *See* Government
    National Mortgage
    Association (GNMA)
Global downturn, 25-28, 54
Global economic depression,
    98-99
Gold, 176
Gould, Joseph, 242
Government:
    agency culture, 223-24
    civil service, 224-25
    expertise and the nature of
        work, 223
    inefficiency of, 221-22
    overregulation by, 222

regulations, business and,
    143-44
restructuring/downsizing,
    225, 229-33
special interest advocacy
    system, 219-20
statutory deadlines, 222-23
Government National
    Mortgage Association
    (GNMA), 48
Government sector, 19-20
Granny dumping, 110
Grippo, Joseph, 124
Gross national product (GNP),
    6, 28, 39, 42, 81, 90
"Group Memory" flip charts,
    creativity sessions, 249
Growth opportunities, See
    Business and growth
    opportunities
Guaranteed investment
    contracts (GICs), 50-51
Guests/onlookers, at creativity
    sessions, 248

H

Handy, Charles, 121-23
Harrison, Bennett, 213
Health care, 13, 31, 100,
    109-10, 214, 229
    job opportunities in, 183,
    190
Heilbroner, Robert, 216
High-IQ organizations, 121-23
High technology sector, 8-9,
    42, 72-73
    See also Computer industry
Honda Motor Company, 19,
    66-67
Hot growth companies,
    warning about, 131-32
Housing costs, 42
Humor, creativity sessions
    and, 252

I

IBM (International Business
    Machines), 4, 8-9, 24-25,
    72, 132
Idea searches, 123-24
Immigrants, 103
"Incubator businesses" units,
    124-25
Independent sector, 240-41
Inflation, 42
Information services, 190
Initial public offering (IPO),
    158
Innovation Search Program
    (SRI), 124
Insurance, job opportunities
    in, 187
Insurance companies, 49-52
Interaction, increasing, 124
Interest-holding techniques,
    creativity sessions, 250
Interest rates, 45
International
    competitiveness, lack of, 2-6
International marketplace,
    growth of, 144-45
International Search
    Association (ISA), 197
Interview tips, 208-10
Investment climate, 37-54
Investments, 147-78
    assets, liquidating, 148-49
    banks, selecting, 153-54
    in chilly investment
        climate, 162-72
    collectibles, 176
    debt reduction, 151-53
    divestitures, 177
    gold, 176
    lack of, 11-13
    portfolio, 154-62
    real estate, 172-76
    savings, 149-50
    small businesses, 176-77
    stockpiling, 177-78

J

Japan:
  auto success, 55-67
  European market and, 26
  investment activity, 4, 144
  quality control, 7, 67
  See also Automobile
    industry; Computer
    industry; High
    technology; Mergers and
    acquisitions
Jevons, William, 81
Job creation companies,
  196-97
Job cuts, ripple effect of, 11, 27
Job prospects, identifying, 205
Job search tips, 198-99, 201-4
  employment profile,
    improving, 202-3
  identify job prospects, 205
  interviews, 208-10
  letters/resumes, 207-8
  major accomplishments,
    listing, 204
  perfect job, identifying,
    203-4
  selling yourself, 204
  strategize, 205-7
  take stock, 201-2
Juglar cycles, 80
Junior college education, 181
Junk bonds, 48-49
Just-in-time (JIT) inventories,
  135

K

Kaufman, Herbert, 218
Kirkland, Lane, 41-42
Kitchin Cycle, 79-80
Kondratieff, Nicolai, 80

L

Laddered portfolio of U.S.
  Treasury Notes, 164-65

Layoffs:
  handling, 199-201
  warning signs of, 199
Lee, Robert J., 192-96
Legal reform, need for, 233-34
Lending, avoiding, 152
Leveraged buyouts (LBOs),
  188
Levi Strauss & Company, 107
Liberal arts education,
  rethinking, 80-81
Lifestyles of customers, 141
Linsenmayer, Adrienne, 70
Little Dragons, 24

M

McDonnell Douglas
  Corporation, 19
McPherson, Joseph, 88, 124
Macro measures, reliance on,
  81-84
Makings of Public Policy, The
  (Dahl), 243
Management:
  in the econoquake, 126
  job opportunities in, 185
  short-sightedness of, 114-19
Management-by-objectives
  (MBO) view, 115-16
Management Horizons, 71
Managerial jobs, decline in
  number of, 20-22
Manufacturing sector, 6-9, 16,
  55-75
  declining jobs in, 19
  foreign production by, 25
  job opportunities in, 187
Marketing expenses, cutting,
  134
Market-oriented
  entrepreneurial firms,
  future and, 238-39
MCI, 123
Medical insurance expenses,
  cutting, 134-35
Mergers and acquisitions,
  9-11, 74, 188

banks, 26, 69-70
Michigan Modernization
    Service (MMS), 237
Middle-class living standards,
    fall in, 22
Minkin Affiliates, 137
Minorities, 101-3
    unemployment among, 23
Mitchell, Wesley C., 80-81, 82
Moderate- to high-risk
    investments, 157-59
    common stocks, 157-58
    preferred stocks, 158-59
Monarch Insurance, collapse
    of, 50
Money market mutual funds,
    155-56
Monsanto Corporation, 123
Monsen, R. Joseph Jr., 222
Municipal bonds, 48-49
Mutual funds, 155-56, 163-64

N

Naisbitt, John, 38, 86
National Aeronautics and
    Space Administration
    (NASA), culture at, 223-24
National Bureau of Economic
    Research (NBER), 79
Networking, 206-7
New Social Marketplace—
    Notes on: Effecting Social
    Change in America's Third
    Century (Crane), 239
Niche marketing, 128-29, 132,
    139-40, 144
1930s:
    banks in, 34
    government policy making
        in, 33
    recession in, 32
    tax collection in, 32
    unemployment
        compensation in, 33
1990s:
    banks in, 34-35
    compared to 1930s, 31-35
        government policy making
        in, 33
    investment climate, 37-54
    recession in, 32
    tax collection in, 32-33
    unemployment
        compensation in, 33-34
Noncallable bonds, 162

O

Odwalla Juice Company, 137,
    141
Ohmae, Kenichi, 121
Older Americans, 108-12
One Hundred Businesses You
    Can Start for $100, 136
Organizational structure,
    reviewing, 133
Organized labor, 218-19
Outplacement psychologist,
    career advice from, 192-96
Overbuilding, 70-72
Overhead, reducing, 132-33
Overregulation by
    government, 222

P

Painter, Jack, 129-30
Patrick, John E., 166-67
Pension Benefits Guaranty
    Corp. (PBGC), 50
Pension funds, 49-52
Perfect job, identifying, 203-4
Personal savings, decline in,
    53
Personnel supply services, job
    opportunities in, 184-85
Peters, Tom, 221, 223, 236-37
Petterson, Al, 173
Pinball psychology, 232
Planning issues, developing,
    142
Politics, 108
Portfolio, 154-62
    bonds, 161-62

moderate- to high-risk
investments, 157-59
short-term debt
instruments, 154-57
stock market, 159-61
Portman, John C., 12, 70
Preferred stocks, 158-59
Private schools, job
opportunities in, 186
Product development, 129
Product line, improving, 128
Professional jobs, decline in
number of, 20-22
Protectionism, 144, 217
Psychology of unemployment,
22-23
Public schools, job
opportunities in, 186

R

*Reader's Guide to Periodical
Literature, The,* 208-9
Reagan administration, trade
deficit and, 3
"Real Estate: The Gathering
Storm" (Linsenmeyer), 70
Real estate, 43, 45-48, 70-71,
107, 135-36, 172-76
job opportunities in, 187
refinancing, 173-75
selling, 149
Real estate investment trust
(REIT), 8
Real income, 39
baby bust generation, 99
lack of growth in, 28
Rebound/recovery, 40, 42
Rebuilding after the
econoquake, 211-45
Recession, 15-16, 18
government cures for, 40-41
*Reclaiming the American
Dream* (Cornuelle), 240
Regional/state economic
recovery groups, 236-39
Rent concessions, seeking,
135-36

Research, job opportunities in,
185
Residential real estate,
coming wipe-out of, 45-48
Responsive branding strategy,
129
Restructuring/downsizing
government, 225, 229-33
decentralize/privatize
government functions,
232-34
elect politicians committed
to America 2000
program, 230-31
identify federal
responsibilities, 230
use world-class
management talent, 231
vote for mandatory budget
cuts, 233
Resumes, 207-8
Retailers, 20, 71-72
Retail trade, job opportunities
in, 186-87
Retirees, *See* Elderly
Retraining programs, 228
R. H. Macy, 12
Rosen, Charlie, 88
Rosen, Jim, 126-27

S

Savings and loan associations
(S&Ls), 51-52
Savings Association Insurance
Fund (SAIF), 157
Savings cushion, building,
149-51
Schedule, creativity sessions,
251
Schumpeter, Joseph, 218
Service sector, 8, 20, 42,
68-75, 189
job opportunities in, 186-87
1981-82 recession and,
68-70
Shakey the Robot, 88
Sharp (Japan), 9

Short-term debt instruments,
    154-57
  bank money market
    accounts, 157
  bank savings account,
    156-57
  certificates of deposit
    (CDs), 155
  checking accounts, 157
  money market mutual
    funds, 155-56
  Treasury issues, 156
Shultz, George, 220, 221, 225,
    234
Skilled labor, 12, 23-25
Small business:
  investing in, 176-77
  survival of, 132
Smart shopper, becoming, 152
Social marketplace, 241-43
Social security benefits:
  baby-boomers and, 107
  elderly and, 109
Southwestern Bell, 51
Special interest advocacy
    system, 219-20
Stanford Research Institute
    (SRI), 87-90, 115, 120, 124
State economies, 27-28
Statutory deadlines, 222-23
Steel industry, 67-68
  voluntary-restraints
    agreement, 68
Steltenpohl, Greg, 137
Stockbrokers, econoquake
    and, 85-86
Stock dividends, reinvesting,
    151
Stock market, 44-45, 159-61
  back burner strategy, 160
  econoquake slippery slope
    theory, 159
  stocks:
    selecting, 160
    selling, 160-61
Stockpiling, 177-78
Straight-line projections, 78
Strategic alternatives,
    developing, 142-43

Strategic marketing plan,
    developing, 137
Strategic unresponsiveness,
    114
Stride Rite Corporation, 110
Structural shifts, economists'
    failure to see, 84-85
Structural unresponsiveness,
    119

T

Taiwan, 23-25
Tax cuts, 228
Tax-exempt municipal bonds,
    as tax shelter, 48
Tax reform, 234
T-bond index (Lehman
    Brothers, Inc.), 48
Technology sector, 8
Telecommunications, job
    opportunities in, 190
Texas Instruments, 24
*Time, Chance and
    Organizations* (Kaufman),
    218
Time-Warner Corporation, 26
Trade deficit, 2-3, 9
Training, corporations'
    investment in, 12
Transplants, 4-6
Treasury issues, 156
Trickle-down economics, 15
Trump, Donald, 70
Tsongas, Paul, 15
TWA (TransWorld Airlines),
    11

U

Ulmer, Melville, 84
Unemployment, 6-9, 11, 13,
    41, 42-43
  exports and, 73-75
  as global problem, 25-28
  psychology of, 22-23

See also Job search tips;
  Layoffs
Unemployment benefits,
  indefinitely extending, 228
Unions, *See* Organized labor
Unisys Corp., 51
U.S. dollar, weakening of, 3
U.S. Treasuries, investing in,
  48
U.S. Treasury Notes, laddered
  portfolio of, 164-65
U.S. West, Inc., 51
USG Corp., 12

V

Variable expenses, debt
  reduction and, 151
Volkswagen AG, 64-66

W

Wallis, W. Allen, 80
Wall Street, 44-45
  computer use on, 13
  See also Stock market;
    specific investments
WalMart Corporation, 189

Wells Fargo & Co., 69
Westerfield, Putney, 188-92
*What Government Agencies Do
  and Why They Do It*
  (Wilson), 221
White-collar workers,
  unemployment among,
  20-22
Wilson, Charles, 7
Wilson, James Q., 221, 222,
  224
*Winning Performance, The:
  How America's
  High-Growth Midsize
  Companies Succeed*
  (Cavanagh), 121
Women, 101, 104
  elder care and, 109-10
Worldly Philosophers, The
  (Heilbroner), 216

Y

Yuppie shock, 105-6

Z

Zimmerman, Robert, 71-72